M3

Charles Seale-Hayne Library
University of Plymouth
(01752) 588 588
LibraryandITenquiries@plymouth.ac.uk

Before School

Liz and Brian Murphy

Before School

CASSELL
LONDON

CASSELL & CO. LTD.

35 Red Lion Square, London WC1R 4SG
and at Sydney, Auckland, Toronto, Johannesburg,
an affiliate of
Macmillan Publishing Co., Inc.,
New York.

First published 1978

ISBN 0 304 29791 7

Typeset by Inforum Limited, Portsmouth
Printed and bound in Great Britain by
Camelot Press, Southampton

*to Nick, Kate, Jane and Patrick
and with many thanks to
my friends in the playgroups*

Contents

Part 1

1 The First Stages

This book is a practical guide for parents, with lots of ideas and suggestions to help them realize the full potential of their child from birth until the time it goes to school. Doing this will enable the child to start its school life with its mental and physical skills developed, help it to adapt quickly and happily to its new environment, and learn more quickly, more easily, more retentively.

It is a practical guide in the truest sense in that all the equipment needed can be found around any ordinary home or can be quickly and easily improvised. It is also practical in that every suggestion it makes is clearly related to a specific and recognizable stage in the child's development — the parent is never in doubt as to why the suggestion is made and what it is intended to achieve. Finally, it does not make unreasonable demands on the parents' time or patience: it accepts that mothers and fathers may not have the time or even the inclination to spend long hours with their babies. But it is important to add that every moment spent with the child is precious and fun for its own sake.

We place great emphasis on communication because the ability to communicate clearly and precisely is basic to the whole process of learning. If a child can communicate well at the age of five it stands a good chance of growing up into a stable and fulfilled adult. Conversely, if a child has not learned to communicate well by the age of five all the evidence points to an unstable and deprived adulthood. Truly the child is father of the man.

This makes serious sense if it is realized that by the time the normal child is five he has learned the basis of nearly all the important things he needs for survival in the modern world. Month by month and stage by stage he has acquired the physical and intellectual skills that first his family and all too soon society at large will demand from him. He has discovered the reality of the material world, he can reason and form concepts, he can see himself in relation to other people, he is able to understand and control his own emotions and he can communicate. And he is secure because all this extraordinary and intricate process has taken place in the warmth and safety of the home.

The necessity for it can be more easily understood if we examine the contributory factors in more detail:

Discovery of the material world

The child's virgin senses need to be tested and refined. Sight, hearing, touch, taste and smell need to be fostered and developed for the child to understand and appreciate the complex texture of life as it goes on around him.

Reasoning and the formulation of concepts

The child begins to understand cause and effect, sequence, and that his actions have consequences. He can also formulate and retain abstract ideas. All these processes must be encouraged.

Other people

The child must learn that he can venture from the safe familiarity of his own family circle into the fascinating world of other people. He needs to be reassured about this, step-by-step.

Emotions

The child learns to understand and control his own emotions, not to over-react, to come to terms with himself. Irrational fears, too, begin to be brought under control.

Communication

The child must be able to communicate his needs and thoughts effectively and precisely and to understand what other people mean with equal precision. Language is the key to full and fast development.

This sounds like a formidable programme and in many ways it is.

4

Overseeing the transformation of a helpless baby into a lively and articulate schoolchild is bound to be an exacting and often exhausting business. But, as a parent, you have one great ally which makes the whole process of bringing up a child fascinating and infinitely rewarding. This is the child's inexhaustible curiosity about everything, all the time. This unquenchable thirst for information is the true stimulus for learning and lightens the teaching task enormously: the child insists on knowing and you — and everyone else for that matter — are an inexhaustible source of knowledge.

This growing-up process is not steady or regular: it is fitful and irregular, a succession of easily recognized physical stages which inevitably occur in the same order, but by no means over the same period of time. Some children can pass through a stage in weeks: others will take months. All we can say with any certainty is that chronological age is an unreliable indicator of ability. Although it is true that the majority of children have reached certain stages by certain chronological ages it is equally true that thousands of lively and intelligent children do not conform to this pattern. No parent should worry if his or her child takes longer to do certain things than the child next door. Time almost always evens things out.

Physical changes are unmistakable and are always accompanied by a characteristic burst of curiosity.

1) The First Stages

2) Lying down
At this age the baby is physically immobile and his back needs support. He begins to learn how to co-ordinate his hands and eyes and to recognize shapes, colours and sounds.

3) Sitting up
This change in posture gives him a new view of the world and a growing awareness of people. He is especially aware of strangers. He is interested in his food and enjoys simple games.

4) Crawling and standing
This is largely a continuation of the previous stage, but the child now becomes mobile. Curiosity develops fast — and can take the child into danger.

5) Toddling and walking
Another new vision of the world plus a sudden concentration on physical development. There is a greatly improved mastery of balance and the child begins to climb up things.

6) Talking to the family
The mastery of walking is accompanied by a great new surge of discovery. The child begins to enjoy playing with others around him and to chatter to the family. He likes to help his mother.

7) 'I am me'
He begins to discover himself as a person with a will of his own and the need to exercise it. This leads to frustration as he also discovers that he cannot manipulate his environment at will.

8) The Later Stages

9) Making things
His span of concentration has grown enough to enable him to make simple constructions or to perform quite delicate manipulations.

10) Playing with older children
Now he enjoys leaving home for short periods and will play happily with other small children. He likes the stimulus given him by new and unexpected things and people outside the home.

11) Those endless questions
The child understands and can cope with his immediate world and has glimpses of a wider world outside. He tries to fit the two together and wants to know how this is done. He is rapidly building his stock of words and ideas.

12) Ready for school
At this stage the child has gained considerable self-confidence, is friendly and sociable, has a vocabulary of more than two thousand words and a grasp of cause and effect. He can understand abstract ideas and is perfectly ready for school.

These twelve stages form the natural framework for this book and a separate chapter is devoted to each one. They begin with a brief description of the physical and mental changes that have taken place in the child and these are followed by suggestions and examples as to how you can help you child in his most formative years.

The last four chapters do not, in fact, delineate physical advances because once a child can walk, talk and manage all the obvious manipulations like feeding and dressing himself, there are no more big physical advances to be made. The rapid developments which take place between the ages of, say, three and five years are all psychological, i.e., in his understanding of the world and himself and being able to communicate it, his social sense, his sense of right and wrong and so on. To this extent, these chapters can be taken together. But they illustrate such different facets of a child's development that it seemed clearer as well as more convenient to treat them in this way.

The twelve stages mentioned are all marked by distinctive sign-posts — you can see the child pulling himself to his feet, you can see his new-found interest in other small children. What is much more difficult to gauge is the intellectual development which you know is simultaneously taking place. The only reliable measure is language. This is why the importance of speech in a child's development cannot be overstressed. Talk to your baby from its earliest weeks. The reason for this is very simple: the only way a child learns language — the ability to communicate — is by being spoken to. And the earlier he hears speech the earlier he will speak. The earlier he speaks, the earlier he will be able to conceptualise, to reason, to learn.

It is not just a matter of words, of learning that everything and everybody has a name (although this is very important). It is not even that every time you talk to your baby you reinforce the parent-child bond that is so vital for his emotional development. It is that language and intelligence are inextricably connected and the sooner he can understand and begin to use words, phrases, sentences, the sooner he will develop into the sensitive and inquiring little human being that every parent would like. So quite apart from mother-talk, making the loving noises that come instinctively to all mothers, make a point of talking to your baby as often as you can.

You will, of course, do considerably more than talk. From the moment of birth your baby is exposed to the outside world and all the sense-impressions that it has to offer. Sight, hearing, touch, taste and smell — all his senses are continually being stimulated and there is much that you can do to enrich this process. At the same time he is developing physical skills: his powers of co-ordination and manipulation improve all the time. Here again much can be done to help him. We offer suggestions in both these areas.

Quite apart from such specific suggestions, a number of general points need to be made. Children are not learning only when they are consciously taught: they are learning *all the time,* sometimes a number of things simultaneously. For instance, the art of getting on with people cannot be taught. It is absorbed by the child as he discovers for himself how the family works and how he fits into it. This process is hindered if the parents are inconsistent; he is presented with conflicting evidence and this inevitably produces anxiety. So 'no' should always mean 'no' and should always be accompanied by an explanation. If no explanation is given, the child has no guide for its future behaviour.

Wise parents will avoid saying 'no' as often as they can. It is often more sensible to distract a child who is misbehaving by giving it something more interesting to do.

Play is vital. It is the method by which a child learns. It offers him the opportunity to use his imagination and stimulate his curiosity. A cardboard box can be a ship, a car, a cave, a house, a lion, all within an hour. At the same time it can offer endless scope for questions. Why is it shaped like that? Why is it so light? What happens if I tear it? Will it break if I stand on it? A child is working hardest when it is most absorbed in play.

Repetition is important. Pleasure in repeating skills that have been mastered gives confidence when tackling new ones. So if a child advances physically it by no means signifies that he has lost interest in all the activities he enjoyed during his previous stage of development. In fact he may well go on enjoying some of his early baby games — such as clapping games — throughout his first five years.

Don't overdo it. This book is a guide and not an operational manual. Anyone attempting to inflict all the suggestions listed here on their suffering infant would not only end up with a bewildered child but with nervous exhaustion. In any case, children need to be left alone, quietly, so that they can assimilate their experiences. Children do this instinctively and it is not only unwise but harmful if they are over-stimulated during their naturally quiet times. It is also as well to remember that his mother needs her own quiet time too. A tired and irritable parent is no great shakes as a teacher.

At the same time, parents should not expect their child to be passive. A normal, healthy child is curious, outgoing, responsive and almost certainly noisy for at least some of the time, and however tiresome this may be on occasions, parents should be glad that it happens. In fact it is fair to say that a child who is never noisy is a cause for concern and investigation.

The class of home is unimportant. The kind of home is very important indeed. For a child even the poorest and barest home is a treasure trove of mysterious and exciting objects, wonderful sensations and fascinating people. If he has love and security, he'll love to learn. Conversely, the most palatial surroundings and a nursery full of expensive toys will benefit a child nothing if he is denied the love and security he needs. There is, naturally, no prescription for a happy home in this book, but parents should remember that children do not need to understand words to understand a quarrel and they are quick to pick up any tension between their parents. This is not to say that a child should be cocooned from the normal hazards of family life, but that a continual atmosphere of strain will soon transmit itself and result in anxiety and insecurity.

Mother, of course, is the centre of a child's universe. She, literally, gives him life and controls his experiences, and it is to her that he instinctively turns if he is frightened or anxious. When it comes to teaching a child how to learn, patently Mother has the key role. The security she gives him is the base from which he moves outwards into the world, experiments, explores. But Father has a vital role too. He is the challenge, the yardstick, the person whose approval is eagerly sought and whose encouragement gives a stimulus for further adventures in thought and physical action. The child also senses the relationship between his parents and the simple one-to-one relationship that was his first understanding has to adapt itself, become more flexible, more complex. The presence of older children or the arrival of a new one presents another set of problems to the developing child: he suddenly learns that he is not the exclusive possessor of his mother's affections and this naturally rouses strong feelings of resentment and jealousy. Parents have to help the child cope with these new, frightening emotions and even the busiest mother must make time to give individual attention to each of her young children. It pays off.

Busy parents should beware of using television as a continual babyminder. Good as some children's programmes are, it is true to say that even very small children are fascinated by the flickering screen and are content to sit in front of it quietly for hours, and this is certainly at the cost of some damage to their development. Television stimulates only sight and hearing and, moreover, it is a great destroyer of curiosity: the child is a passive spectator and not a participant. A child needs real experiences where all his senses come into play: he needs to know what a horse feels and smells like, to get a first-hand knowledge of the living animal. Television often acts as a barrier even for older children between them and the real world. Too much television can severely inhibit the desire of small children to learn.

Books, on the other hand, are great stimulators of the imagination. Words evoke their own pictures and illustrations can be looked at again and again as a familiar story is told. Moreover looking at a book together involves close physical contact with a child. There is total mutual absorption — the mother's voice, the child's pointing finger, the words of a favourite story — a completely shared experience. As has been said before, the omnipresence of the mother in the child's universe cannot be over-emphasized.

2 Lying Down

The first few days of a baby's life are spent in coming to terms with a whole range of new-found senses and his basic drives. More than ninety per cent of his time is spent asleep and the brief periods when he is awake are spent feeding or demanding to be fed. His universe is bounded by the nipple and the presence of his mother and he has no time or attention for anything else. He needs warmth, quiet and screening from bright light; his social needs are nil. But even at this very early age he will begin to respond to you and as the days pass and he becomes aware of light and sounds it is important to give him plenty of attention when he is awake.

However, at about six weeks he begins to get some control of his arms and the amount of time he is awake increases quite dramatically — to between a quarter and a third of his life. He now has time to develop his interest in the outside world.

First of all, he welcomes as much human contact as possible. He needs to be picked up, cuddled, talked to. This is generally not much of a problem. Not only are the immediate members of his family — father and elder brothers and sisters — eager to pick him up and fuss over him, but grandparents, uncles and aunts and family friends can hardly be restrained. However, a very common pattern is for the novelty of his existence to wear off at about the time his need for people really begins to develop. So make sure he gets as much of your time as possible and encourage your immediate family to keep up the good work. Don't be afraid you will spoil him by giving him attention when he is lying quietly. The more stimulus he gets the quicker he will respond and the quicker he will learn the skills and co-ordination that are essential for the next stage in his development. Handle him firmly and make sure that anyone who picks him up holds him firmly. Babies have an instinctive fear of falling and firm handling reassures them and is good for their sense of security. (Incidentally, a baby's other instinctive fear is the fear of loud noises and he should never be exposed to them.) His head should be firmly supported all the time.

Remember he will not be interested in looking around and paying attention if he is hungry or uncomfortable. So pick your moment; make sure he is fed and dry before you start his first lessons in what the world is all about. It also helps if you establish regularity in his routine: a sense of order, of the same things happening in the same sequence at the same time, helps him to feel secure.

The mouth is the only fully operational sense organ in his earliest months. It is the most sensitive and mature area of his body and anything he is given or gets hold of will be taken straight there. So — obviously — make certain that anything he can reach is safe and that he can't get hold of anything small enough to swallow. Take special care that generous toddlers do not give him unsuitable gifts when your back is turned. This orientation towards the mouth lasts some months before sensitivity migrates to the fingers.

As far as is practicable he should sleep in the same place so that he always wakes up in familiar surroundings. Once he is awake his scenery should vary as much as possible. Take him with you from room to room and don't always put him down in the same place. Then he will continually see something new or something familiar from a new angle. And, of course, if you take him with you it is easier to talk to him or satisfy the natural impulse to pick him up and play with him. This is good for both of you, but especially for him.

Remember that he is incapable of moving and so always see things from the horizontal. You can vary this angle by putting a cushion under him in his cot or pram: this should be done with great care to make sure his back is straight and his head supported, otherwise it is not only uncomfortable but positively bad for him. The best solution, in fact, is to buy one of the 'baby sitters' specially designed for this — a lightweight portable cot with a built-in adjustable slope which tilts him at a comfortable angle and allows him to see a great deal more than he would do otherwise. Or, of course, Father can always improvise with a sheet of plywood nailed to a four-inch block of wood, shaped to fit the base of the cot and placed under the mattress.

This change of locale means that not only is his sense of sight continually stimulated, but so are his other senses. Different rooms produce different sounds — the running water in the bathroom, the clash of pots and pans in the kitchen, the ticking clock in the sitting-room. All this trains and refines his hearing. Rooms also smell different — meaty, fishy, spicy smells in the kitchen, soapy, scented smells in the bathroom, the smell of furniture polish and wellington boots in the hall — any house has a hundred different smells. Recognizing them and detecting the difference helps develop his sense of smell.

Make the most of the incidents that shape his day — being fed, changed, bathed. However busy you are these are times that can be stretched to your mutual pleasure and advantage.

Most of these activities will be carried out by the baby's mother, but there is every reason why the family should join in too. The baby can watch and hear his elder brothers and sisters playing or see his father sawing a plank. And here a familiar word of warning. The mother's natural obsession for her new baby must not blind her to the needs of her other children — nor, indeed, of her husband. Unconscious resentments and jealousies can build up very easily and once established are difficult to eradicate. As far as is possible the mother should include the whole family in the welfare and education of its newest member. Remember also that other members of the family have things to offer that Mother has not — the roughness of Daddy's face and the smell of his clothes (surely one of the earliest and most evocative memories we carry with us from childhood), the laughter of children, the hug of a not-so-big brother. All these things add up to solid advances in his awareness of the world.

Things a lying-down baby needs

Sight
Things to look at around his cot.
Things to look at from his 'baby-sitter'.
Toys near enough for him to look at and touch.

Sound

Being talked to as often as possible by as many people as possible —
but especially his mother.
Sounds associated with different rooms.
Music played specially to listen to, not just as background.
Sounds from different directions.
Being sung to, however inexpertly.
The avoidance of sudden loud noises.

Touch

Things of varying texture in daily use.
Different temperatures.
Variety of textured toys.
Daddy's face.
Water. Splashing in the bath.

Smell

Smells associated with different rooms and different people.
Varied toiletries.
Food and flower smells.

Taste

This will develop as he puts things in his mouth — texture, taste and
shape will be the first sense-experiences he is fully aware of.
Varied diet.

Physical

A baby likes to be firmly wrapped when sleeping but his arms should
be free so that he can see the movements his hands make and learn to
focus his eyes on them.

Hand-eye co-ordination begins when he hits some brightly
coloured object by chance and learns that he can hit it again. During
his waking hours he should have things close enough to help him
develop this co-ordination.

Give him plenty of time to kick and wave his arms unemcumbered
by nappies and heavy clothes. He will move his body about until he is
able to arch his back, lift his head from the mattress, and turn over.
Even if he cries and wants to be on his tummy again he will still continue to practise turning over.

Try to give him at least one exercise time a day. However busy you are he will respond more vigorously if you are around. If you have to leave him for a moment, make sure he is safe — the new skill of rolling over can be acquired very quickly.

Social

A new baby is very much a centre of attraction to many people. But remember it is the constant presence of his mother that gives him his basic security.

Involve all the family in his waking moments so that they become familiar and comforting figures and he will quickly learn to respond to them too.

Practical suggestions

Sight

Mobiles

These are something he can look at when he is by himself in his cot or pram. They can be hung with threads of cotton pinned or stuck to the ceiling and they need not be elaborate. These are some excellent mobile kits, but home-made ones are just as effective.

Suggestions for mobiles

Baubles and bells from the Christmas tree.

Crumpled kitchen foil.

Sparkly costume jewellery.

Shapes made from coloured paper.

Bird. Cut a bird shape and staple long strips of coloured tissue paper to form a tail.

Spiral of paper cut from a circle.

Figures. Cut from a circle of paper and decorate with strips of tissue paper or foil.

Cut a bird shape
Staple long strips
of coloured paper
to form a tail

cut a circle
as shown to
form a mobile

figure cut from a circle
of paper

decorate with strips of
paper or foil

Christmas tree baubles

and costume jewellery

Cradle toys

For the few months that a baby sleeps in a cradle or carry-cot it is often very difficult to string things across — there are no projections to tie them to. The answer is to tie a stick to the side of the cot so that you can attach some bright objects to it — a bouncy doll on elastic which will bob when the baby moves, shiny glass beads that catch the light, a plastic mug, crumpled shiny foil, coloured feathers, coloured paper shapes, anything bright. It is very easy to improvise. When he is able to touch them make sure there is nothing small enough to swallow.

Cradle toys

17

Pram rattle

Strings of large bright plastic beads can be bought to put across the pram. You can make your own by painting cotton reels (with lead-free paint) and stringing them on firm elastic. Thread a budgie-bell at each end so that they tinkle when the toy is touched.

Thread painted cotton reels onto a length of elastic with a budgie bell at each end

Bouncing bird

It is possible to buy a plastic bird on a long spring that can be attached by a suction-cup to the ceiling. Start the bird bouncing and it will continue for nearly half an hour.

Pictures

A baby is usually given nothing but a blank wall to stare at. Instead, hang one of your own favourite pictures for him to look at or pin a pop poster to the wall or ceiling, changing it occasionally. Your own abstract picture made out of large coloured squares is fun to make and very effective. Make sure there is always something on the wall to look at.

Window-sill

Put a coloured glass vase on the window-sill where the baby can see it. Place it where the light shines through it. A jam jar wrapped in coloured cellophane will have the same effect — or a jar filled with coloured marbles.
A fish tank with fish swimming in it will attract his attention when he begins to focus.

Lampshade

A pretty lampshade with a not very bright light-bulb will catch his eye. Make sure no strong direct light reaches his eyes.

Sound

Talk to your baby

He can only learn to talk back to you by imitating the sounds he hears. Ask the family and anyone else near him to talk to him too. Sing to your baby. Nursery rhymes, pop songs, anything that comes into your head.

Baby rhymes

Rhymes which involve his body are excellent and enjoyable for both. Some well-known examples are:

This little piggy went to market	Touch big toe or finger
This little piggy stayed at home	Touch second toe or finger
This little piggy had roast beef	Touch third toe or finger
This little piggy had none	Touch fourth finger
This little piggy went 'wee-wee-wee-wee' all the way home	Run the finger rapidly up arm or leg and quickly tickle some appropriate spot

Walkie round the garden	Make circles on the baby's palm with a finger.
Like a teddy bear	
One step	'Walk' finger up arm
Two steps	Another step
Tickly under there!	A quick tickle under the arm

Clock

Show him a clock. Let him listen to it. Put a clock beside his cot occasionally.

Music

Play records or put on the radio. Try not to get him used to it as background, but as something to listen to specifically.

Wind chimes

These are small mobiles made of thin blades of glass or metal which touch each other and tinkle when the wind moves them. They come in kits and are quite cheap. But they can be improvised from any small pieces of thin metal (such as the insides of an old clock) pierced and strung on cotton.

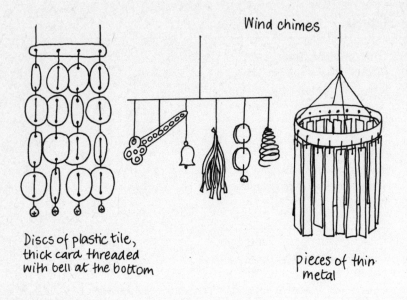

Wind chimes

Discs of plastic tile,
thick card threaded
with bell at the bottom

pieces of thin
metal

Room sounds

Your baby will soon learn to distinguish rooms by their different
sounds. Make sure he has the maximum opportunity to do this by
putting him as close to the source of the sound as is practicable, as
long as it is not too loud.

Out-of-door sounds

Sound is, of course, only one of the sensations of being out of doors.
A baby looks up to see the changing shapes of house, trees, clouds
(but keep his eyes out of direct sunlight). He smells the grass, the
smoke, town and country smells. He feels the cold wind, the warm
sun. He also hears a whole set of fascinating new sounds. Let him
hear them as often as he can.

Touch

Toys with different textures
This is just a start to a toy box which should be as varied as possible.

Velvet fish
Cut out two fish shapes in velvet, about eight inches long. Cut out an extra piece of tail in a piece of heavy fabric like sheeting or corduroy. Stitch this extra piece of tail to the wrong side of one of the fish pieces. Then with right sides facing stitch round the whole of the fish leaving a small opening at the side. Turn the fish so the right side is outside. Stitch the tail as illustrated. Stuff with scraps of nylon or bits of clean rag. Sew up opening. Embroider an eye on each side.

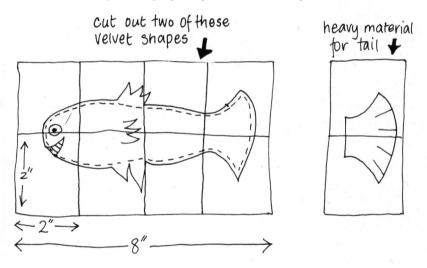

cut out two of these velvet shapes ↓

heavy material for tail ↓

2″

←2″→

←——————— 8″ ———————→

Smell and taste
These go very much together at this early stage. But there is every reason to let a child taste different things, smell different things. So vary his diet occasionally to let him experience new tastes and flavours. It is easy to expose him to new smells too. Lemons and other fruit have interesting smells and most household cupboards will disclose something interesting.

He'll like the reassuring familiarity of his own toiletries but, again, don't be frightened of varying these occasionally. And remember that Mother herself is a rich source of smells — her own physical ones of skin, breath and milk as well as the scent of her soap and perfumes.

Physical

Exercise time
Every day a baby should be left in a warm safe place, without nappies, to kick his legs, wave his arms and develop his hand-eye co-ordination. Here he will practise the essential movements of head-lifting, back-arching and rolling over.

Touching things
During the few months before he is able to sit up he will learn to see and touch objects. You can encourage him with cot and pram mobiles and with bright attractive things to catch hold of.

Social
Mother is definitely the centre of his world. She provides food, comfort and security. Regular contact with Father and brothers and sisters starts to widen his view of the world. A smiling baby always gets an attentive audience.

3 Sitting Up

When a baby first begins to sit up he is not very stable. He will need you with him to pick him up when he rolls over and to give him encouragement and praise for his new skill. He will also need support for his back, although he will be able to sit unsupported for short periods.

He has learned to reach out and pick things up and turn them over in his hand. He will shake things about and, of course, everything he picks up will be carried to his mouth so that he can experience its taste and texture. His new posture gives him a new view of the world; he can look around him and pick up toys when he sits on a rug on the floor. He can sit in his pram and see what is going on, he can see things and people approaching and departing and he can learn the game of leaning out and dropping things over the side. At mealtimes he will join the family, sitting strapped into his high chair. He will begin to socialize properly, although he will still like being cuddled by Mummy when he is being given his bottle. Bathtime is great fun with plenty of splashing and laughter.

It is not difficult to see that all this activity will quickly lead to the crawling stage when he will be able to get at the things that are now so infuriatingly out of reach. There is an increasing amount of evidence that this crawling stage is vital to the development of a baby's intelligence because it is all about the co-ordination of his eyes and his bodily movements. Once he can sit firmly by himself you can encourage him to begin crawling by putting him on his hands and knees. Once he has got the idea he will not need showing again.

It is when he is sitting up that the first primitive experiments of cause and effect are made. The toy will fall — and *always* fall — if dropped. Gravity becomes a reliable constant in his life because he tests it countless times until he understands and accepts it.

At this age toys do not have to be elaborate. He will need a couple of good safe rattles that can be turned around in his hands, shaken and bitten, a bunch of teething rings of various colours, a squeaky toy in plastic or rubber and a soft woolly animal. Improvised toys can be just as effective — a spoon in a tin (with no sharp edges), a ball of tissue paper in a box, a box with a hinged lid that can be opened and shut.

Things a sitting-up baby needs and does

Sight

Make sure the walls of the room where he sleeps have bright pictures or patterns on them that will catch his attention when he wakes up. Suspended cot toys and mobiles continue to be useful: change them from time to time.

Now that he is sitting up he will have much more opportunity and incentive to look around him. See that he has something interesting to look at when he is left on his own and is not left to stare at a blank wall.

Sound

Let him have things to play with that have a particular noise of their own — a rattle, a drum, dried peas in a sealed cardboard box, a small bell. He will be interested in where sounds come from. Show him. Play 'where am I?' games with him, calling his name from different directions so that he has to turn his head to find you.

Touch

Touch now becomes very important. He is still learning about objects by carrying them to his mouth and tongue but this sensitivity gradually transfers itself to his fingers. Eventually he will be able to judge the shape and texture of an object just by looking at it, but at this stage of his development everything has to be experienced directly.

Make sure his toys have different textures. Let him have toys that are soft, hard, flexible, smooth, rough, fluffy, rubbery and so on. And don't forget shape. Give him the basic geometrical solids — cubes, balls, cones, discs and squares — in a variety of colours. These will be useful throughout his entire early childhood and you cannot begin collecting them too soon.

Smell and taste

He should continue to experience the indoor smells he is familiar with and to these are now added a whole range of outdoor ones. His sense of smell is becoming more discriminating all the time so let him have as much variety as you can.

Everything he can grab will be carried straight to his mouth so he will inevitably experience a range of tastes that adults are usually unaware of — rubber, wood, plastic, wool, etc., as well as his normal diet. See that his diet is varied and that when he begins to teethe he gets a variety of rusks to bite and chew on.

Now that he can sit up he will begin to take more interest in his food. Sometimes he will not want to eat, but this problem can be solved by drawing his attention to some bright object and literally slipping the food into his mouth when he is not looking. Small babies find it very difficult to concentrate on more than one thing at a time.

He will graduate to a plastic cup in his own good time; he may prefer to cuddle down with a bottle for quite a while. His sense of smell and taste are developing rapidly and he will now decisively reject certain foods and drinks because he has decided he does not like them. This is nothing to worry about. In fact, quite the reverse, because it proves his senses are developing properly. Make sure he encounters as many tastes as possible.

Give him pieces of food to hold and play with, e.g. a segment of orange, a ginger biscuit, a piece of bread and butter. Don't forget that if you give him a rose he won't smell it, he will eat it!

When he is watching you in the kitchen, let him smell the things you are using — fruits, herbs, spices, fish, vegetables. And remember that many three-year-olds say 'nasty' when they experience a strong smell because they are unable to associate it with its taste.

Physical

His back is now strong enough to hold his head up and his co-ordination is markedly better. He will begin to enjoy using his body. He can reach out for things and hold them with both hands, he exercises energetically on his back, arching, kicking, pushing his hand against the end of his cot, rolling over. On his tummy he can bring his knees under him, raise his head and feet simultaneously and move round in a circle. When he sits on your lap he can push himself up into a standing position, and be obviously enjoys doing this.

If you have to leave him for a few moments make sure that he is safe; he can roll over quite unexpectedly and this could be dangerous. If you do not have much space and are worried about someone tripping over him, use a playpen.

Social

Your baby is now beginning to respond very positively to sound. He can differentiate between different tones of voice and will respond with noises of his own. These can easily be distinguished as expressing eagerness or anger. He will show interest in his father's voice and in the familiar voices of his brothers and sisters and other people he often sees. Most of all, of course, he is tremendously responsive to his mother's voice.

He holds out his arms when you go to pick him up and he enjoys bouncing games. At the same time a great deal of consolidation is going on. He will need to be left on his own quite frequently, surrounded by familiar toys which he can pick up and turn over in his hands, perfecting his hand and eye co-ordination.

You will have noticed that from a few weeks old your baby has been making little noises to himself. From the time he can sit up firmly by himself he will begin to organize these random and experimental sounds into a primitive language. He will try to imitate the noises he hears around him. These little gurgles resolve themselves into 'bbb' 'ggg' 'ddd' sounds, but his mother's very positive response to the 'mm mm' and 'dd dd' sounds will lead him to repeat them with increasing vigour and confidence. This is the birth of speech.

So talk to your baby. He cannot practise his first words unless he hears them from you.

Other people

He now begins to love company and the attention people give him, and his pleased reaction to their noticing him encourages them to play with him and talk to him. Without being neurotic about it, make sure that he sees a good many people and that they talk to him and make a fuss of him. Oddly enough, this bright and happy sociability will disappear during his next stage of development — and for very sound reasons — but while he is sitting up it needs encouraging. Not that talking to and playing with a smiling and responsive baby is any great penance.

Practical suggestions

Sight

Shapes

Start a collection of different shapes, sizes and colours. They can be made from quarter-inch-thick wood or plywood. Cut out a square, a circle, a triangle, a rectangle. Point them different colours. As the child develops you can add to this basic collection with more unusual shapes, extra colours and different sizes. Remember to smooth all edges and to use lead-free paint.

N.B. Don't throw away the pieces of wood you cut the shapes from. It comes in very useful later (see page 185).

Paint the shapes in different colours
Cut out another set, exactly the same, but change the colours round. Keep the board you cut them from.

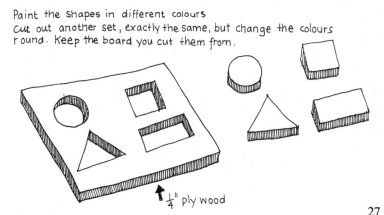

↑ ¼" ply wood

Mirror
A small unbreakable mirror with a hard rubber frame will catch his eye and interest him continually.

Mobiles
Remember to change the mobiles in the baby's room occasionally. Here are a few more suggestions:
Fish shapes cut from coloured cellophane
Silver mice with tinsel tails
Coloured woolly pom-poms.

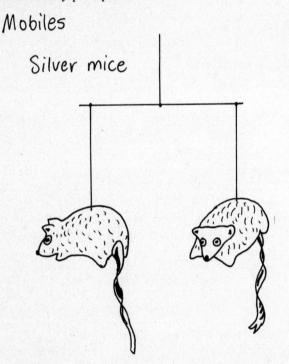

Mobiles

Silver mice

Use a ball of aluminium foil, crush it into a mouse shape. Stick a 6" piece of tinsel for a tail. Stick on two buttons for eyes.

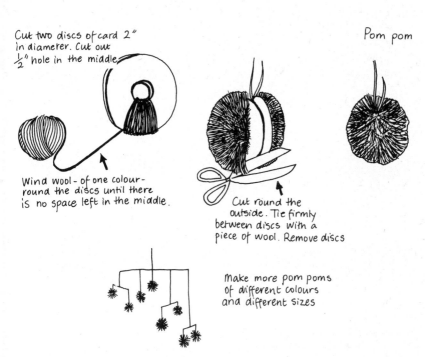

Cut two discs of card 2" in diameter. Cut out ½" hole in the middle.

Pom pom

Wind wool - of one colour - round the discs until there is no space left in the middle.

Cut round the outside. Tie firmly between discs with a piece of wool. Remove discs

Make more pom poms of different colours and different sizes

Room where baby sleeps

See that the walls, the sides of the cot and even the ceiling have something interesting to look at on them. This can often be done by placing the cot intelligently — most rooms have a corner with something visually exciting in it. The cot should also have something interesting to touch within reach. The idea is that he should always have something stimulating to look at and touch.

Pot plants

Put a bowl with bulbs in it on the window-sill. Some flowers — like hyacinths — have a beautiful heavy scent as well as blooms. Let your baby experience both. Flowers in a vase are also a good idea. Natural flowers are better than plastic not only because they smell nicer and have a pleasanter texture but because you have to change them!

Bath toys

Bright plastic floating toys, ducks, balls, etc. Make sure that things like boats don't have sharp masts or projections. Plastic cups and spoons are fun to play with. At the sitting stage a baby will still need support in the bath, but he can sit firmly and enjoy splashing about in the water.

Rooms in the house

Continue taking him with you from room to room whenever you can. (Obviously the kitchen may be difficult but even this can be managed sometimes.) He will sit on a rug on the floor and with a few toys to hand he will be perfectly happy. He should always face into the room, never at a blank wall.

Out-of-doors

Pushing a pram is much more fun now that the baby can take an active interest in what is going on around him. He will need support at first and should not be left sitting up long until his back is really strong. He should be taken out as often as possible for every kind of reason — the sights, sounds and smells of town and country are a perpetual feast of novelty and he will use these new sensations as stimuli for his growing involvement in the outside world.

Sound

Rattle

There are a great many attractive rattles on the market and many babies are given more than they can cope with by relations and family friends. Some of the best are the ones he can see into, made of transparent plastic with coloured shapes inside which bounce about. Another attractive type is in wood with a bell that can be touched through the sides. Make sure they are well made and chew-proof. Some can be dangerous if broken.

Drum

A biscuit tin and wooden spoon make a perfect drum. This is one toy the baby can play with all by himself.

Radio

Your baby will enjoy listening to the music you like. Try not to leave the music on purely as background noise: this will result in his losing the sharpness and clarity of other pleasant household noises and hearing only a diffuse and continual buzz. But if you obviously respond to what you hear by singing, humming or tapping, the baby will respond to your enjoyment.

Record player

The advantage of a record player is that you can choose exactly what you want to listen to. At this age you need not bother about special baby records. He will enjoy what you enjoy. Vary your musical diet as much as possible and you will vary his at the same time. Using your record player when your baby is this age is a pleasure for both of you and it will be an invaluable aid to you a little later in his childhood.

Room sounds

If you can manage to sit down quietly during the day, stop for a few moments and listen. You will then hear the sounds your baby hears — the ticking of the clock, the whir of the washing machine, the noise of a lorry passing, water running, the dog scratching. You too contribute noises to your baby's hearing — washing up, opening and shutting doors, polishing, singing, walking about, picking things up and putting them down again. Your baby's waking hours are accompanied by a rich fabric of sounds and he is beginning to relate them to the people and objects that make them.

Touch

Finger ball

This is a soft plastic ball with ridges all over the surface that is easy to pick up and play with and does not roll away very easily. It is excellent for making your baby aware that his fingers can detect differences as well as his mouth.

Bean bag

A bean bag made in an interesting shape and loosely filled with dried haricot beans, dried peas or lentils will have a fascinating feel as it flops about in your baby's hands.

Make it in strong, firm cotton using the smallest possible machine stitch. If you use buttons for eyes make sure they are sewn on very strongly or they will soon be picked or sucked off. It is better to embroider them.

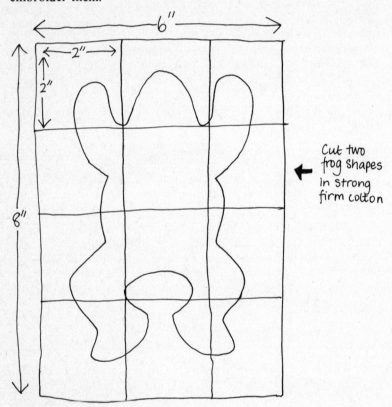

Cut two frog shapes in strong firm cotton

Prickly hairbrush

Make sure this is quite clean. Wash it first in warm detergent and rinse carefully. He will be fascinated with the feel of a hairbrush and its extraordinary prickles, quite unlike the warm soft objects that surround him.

Fur

Add to his collection of toys by making something out of a scrap of fur. If you are making a small furry animal, such as a rabbit, make sure the 'nap' is in the right direction, i.e., from head to tail, so that it can be stroked as it would be in real life.

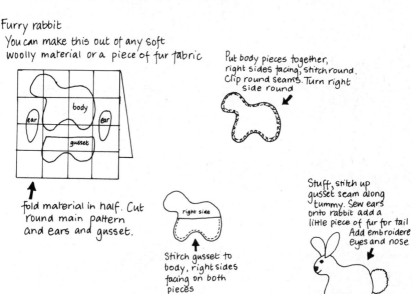

Furry rabbit
You can make this out of any soft woolly material or a piece of fur fabric

fold material in half. Cut round main pattern and ears and gusset.

Put body pieces together, right sides facing, stitch round. Clip round seams. Turn right side round

Stitch gusset to body, right sides facing on both pieces

Stuff, stitch up gusset seam along tummy. Sew ears onto rabbit add a little piece of fur for tail. Add embroidere eyes and nose

Cot mobile

Look again at the toys suspended over his cot. He will now be able to reach out and grab them and they should be adapted to this new ability. Attach things with different textures as well as different colours and shapes — velvety, hard, rubbery, furry.

If he has graduated to a drop-side cot, tie a stick across and suspend a similar array of objects from it on lengths of elastic. Your household is full of suitable things — a plastic bracelet, a teaspoon, a rattle, a child's glove.

Things about the house

Your baby will now begin to enjoy the moments when you carry him about the house and stop occasionally to let him touch things. He will sit up attentively in your arms, reach out and make little noises. Talk about what he is touching, name it and describe it to him. Babies are never too young to listen to words and the way in which they are used.

Smell and taste

Pieces of food
Pieces of food with a distinctive smell and taste and large enough for him to hold are a good idea. A wedge of turnip or cauliflower stalk, a ginger biscuit or a piece of hard cheese. Don't give him something that will crumble in his mouth because he might choke on it.

Physical

Exercise
He needs a warm, safe place to exercise his body without being hampered by his nappy. He is best on a hard surface, preferably on a rug on the floor. He'll enjoy this best if you watch and encourage him, play with his toes, turn him over when he rolls and let him kick against your knees.

Posting
A box and a ball of paper are good enough. But he'll enjoy putting a brick into a tin. This is all practice for his fingers.

Knotted cord
A piece of dressing-gown cord knotted at intervals is fascinating for him. Attach it to the side of his cot or playpen, but do not let him have it long enough to get tied up in.

Social

Peep-bo

This is a game your baby will love. Hide your face behind your hands and then reveal it — suddenly, saying 'Bo'. At this age he will not understand that you have not, in fact, disappeared. The only things that have reality are those things he can actually see, hear or touch. When you reappear smiling his response to the fun will be immediate. Variations of this game are innumerable — hiding behind a door, disappearing behind a sheet when making the bed, vanishing behind a curtain — your own ingenuity and domestic geography will teach you.

Action rhymes
Sit baby on your lap and tap the soles of his feet as you say:
>Shoe a little horse
>Shoe a little mare
>But let the little colt go bare, bare bare.

Sit baby on your lap and bounce him up and down very gently at first and then with more gusto, ending up with letting him fall between your knees:
>This is the way the ladies ride
>Trottety, trottety, trot
>This is the way the gentlemen ride
>Bumpety, bumpety, bump
>And this is the way the farmers ride
>Gallopy, gallopy, gallop
>And down in the ditch!

4 Crawling and Standing

One day, probably when you are least expecting it, you will find that the baby you left sitting quietly on his rug has moved some distance away from it. This startling venture marks the beginning of the most exciting (and, for you, exhausting) eighteen months of his life. Within an astonishingly short time those first few tentative little forays from the familiar safety of his rug will have developed into fast and confident exploration of everywhere his hands and knees will take him. He will be off after every bright and interesting object that catches his attention and attain a turn of speed that is almost unbelievable. At about the same time he will also be attracted to objects that he cannot reach from his all-fours position and he will try to grab them by pulling himself to his feet — an activity he was preparing for when he pushed his legs against yours and the end of his cot. Crawling and standing go very much together.

These first few crawling months are fascinating because your baby is developing so quickly. But they are also extremely demanding because he is quite undiscriminating and has absolutely no sense of danger. Just as a few months previously he would have unhesitatingly taken poison straight to his mouth, now he will get to and grab anything that catches his eye — plastic toy, dropped spoon, kitten or live electric wire. The only sensible answer is to clear a room or part of a room of everything that is dangerous, fragile or valuable so that he can investigate everything without constantly being told 'No'.

He must be encouraged to be curious, to touch and probe, to bang and shake the things he finds. This is one of the main ways in which he learns about the world around him. If he has had plenty to occupy him in his first six months he will be naturally active and inquisitive and not frightened of new sights and new objects. If you now begin to stop him touching things he will work out that it is somehow wrong to be curious and this will make him very confused. Keep things he should not touch well out of his way.

Crawling is essential to the development of his intelligence. It involves enormous improvements in his physical co-ordination, widens his sensory horizons and gives him a new understanding of space and dimension. He should be encouraged to crawl and explore to the limit, however tempting the idea is of leaving him in his playpen or cot because then you do not have to watch him all the time. Playpens are perfectly acceptable for short periods or for specific occasions — you have to answer the telephone and go to the lavatory occasionally — but as a substitute for the ever-changing world of the floor they are a poor second best. And if you have to leave your baby with a baby-minder or relative, make sure they understand the necessity of letting him have the free crawl of a substantial area of floor. Babies soon become bored and lethargic if they spend all their time cooped up in a small space. So would you.

Your baby, of course, will not be crawling all his waking hours. He will need — and take — periods of consolidation when he sits quietly playing with familiar toys or examining new ones. What was said in the last chapter continues to be true, although many of his baby habits — like taking everything to his mouth — will begin to fall away from him.

Safety

This is the most dangerous age for a child. He is surrounded by lethal objects and locations and he has no judgement, no experience. The home is a place of joy and security and of great and unknown danger. It is essential that everywhere he goes is safe for his curiosity and exploration. So take no risks. A child howling in a playpen is better than no child at all. Make sure all the following points are fully covered.

Electric plugs

Make sure all sockets are of childproof design or else fit tight plugs in them. Those little holes are fascinating to little fingers or, worse, for little fingers holding little bits of metal.

Flex

Most plugs have wires attached to them. If your baby finds it, it will be pulled. If it is connected to an electric iron or electric kettle . . . So make quite certain that your baby cannot get at it.

Ironing

This is obviously one of the jobs you can do while your baby crawls around the room. However, although it is the easiest thing in the world to pop out for just a second to refill the sprinkler or something similar, don't do it. Take your baby with you to watch and listen to you filling the sprinkler instead.

Electric kettle, percolator etc.

These are far too dangerous to leave within his reach even if you are with him all the time. No one can watch a baby every second of the time and they move very, very quickly. Keep kettles and percolators well out of reach.

Fires

It is against the law to have an unguarded fire in the same place as a small child. For sombre reasons: every year more than a hundred children under five die of burns or scalds received at home. Nearly five thousand from England and Wales alone are burned or scalded in the home severely enough to go into hospital. Many more more receive painful, frightening burns or scalds. No parent wants its child burnt, but thousands each year are careless enough to allow it to happen. All it needs is a moment's inattention.

Don't let it happen to your child! Keep all fires completely and securely guarded with fire guards that are firmly attached to the fireplace. They should be completely enclosed so that the child cannot throw things over the top. A good fire guard is quite cheap and buys you peace of mind for many years. Gas and electric fires must be similarly guarded.

Cookers

The projecting handle of a saucepan is there to be grabbed and pulled. Make sure that you — and anyone else who uses the cooker — keep all handles turned in. Better, buy one of the special attachments that can be fitted to your cooker and lock saucepan handles safely — inquire for particulars at a gas or electricity showroom.

Poisons

Every year more than thirty children die of poisons they take in the home. Every year nearly ten thousand children in England and Wales alone poison themselves in the home badly enough to have to stay in hospital. Not only drugs and medicines, but a great many normal household products — cleaners, bleaches, polishes, sprays, toiletries, detergents, garden fertilizers, etc — are dangerously poisonous. If you don't know this, your baby doesn't either. And he wants to experiment. If it is liquid, he'll drink it. If it can be eaten, he'll eat it. It actually happens to thousands of children every year.

Don't let it happen to your child! Keep all drugs and medicines in a high medicine cupboard and keep it locked or tightly closed. Keep all kitchen and household products well out of his reach. And don't forget it won't be long before he can drag a chair over, climb on it and reach that so-called inaccessible shelf and those delicious-looking bottles and jars. So if you keep your bleach and furniture polish in the cupboard under the sink, move them *today*. Tomorrow may be too late. The moment he starts climbing, make sure that shelf really can't be reached. Don't forget he'll be into *every* room. Where do you keep your lavatory cleaner . . . ?

Plastic bags

Keep them out of his reach. Explain why when he is a little older. Don't forget that suit covers from dry-cleaners and a number of seemingly harmless packets and coverings are potentially lethal. They can suffocate a small child in a few seconds.

Sharp things

Make sure Daddy puts his razor away and does not throw old blades into the waste bin. Make sure that you don't leave kitchen or carving knives about. Most households have other sharp things in use which are dangerous — scissors, screwdrivers, opened tins, pins and needles. Don't get neurotic about it but make sure they are kept out of reach.

Glass and crockery

Harmless when whole but easily broken. Don't put them down carelessly so that they can easily be knocked over. Never give your baby a glass to drink from unless you are holding it too. Let him have a plastic cup until he is of school age. Milk bottles break easily, as do glass ashtrays and vases.

Low tables

Keep them clear of dangerous objects. He will eat cigarette ends. He will break cups and glasses that are left on them. He will tear paper out of expensive books too, which may not present a hazard to your baby but might present one to your own blood pressure.

Tablecloths

Cause and effect again. If you pull it, it will come down. He will pull it and it will come down — including the freshly brewed pot of tea. Keep the edges of tablecloths out of his reach and don't forget that if a chair is by the table he will use it to pull himself up. He can then reach more than two feet up in the air.

Stairs

It is wise to fix a child-proof gate at the top and bottom of any flight of stairs your baby is likely to encounter at home. If this is impossible you can improvise by turning a small table on its side or putting up some similar temporary barrier. Make sure this is firm and cannot be pulled over or got round. Crawling babies are stronger than you think and can wiggle their little bodies through astonishingly narrow gaps. One final tip: keep the stairs clear of discarded toys. Not for the baby's sake, but for your own and everybody else's.

Windows

Make sure that your baby cannot scramble up to windows by chair, sofa or other climbable object and that the lower window frames are locked or very firmly closed, particularly if you live in a flat or upstairs. Keep this up until your child is old enough to realize that it is dangerous to lean out of high windows.

Outside fences and gates

A garden is ideal for a baby to crawl (and later to toddle) in, full of exciting objects, smells and other sensations. But it must have a secure fence and gate. Your own garden may be perfectly safe, but the one next door and, more important, the road outside, may be full of danger. And remember that postmen, milkmen and other visitors don't automatically shut the gate.

Water

If you have a pond in your garden, cover it securely with wire netting. Water has a tremendous attraction for children and a small child can drown in amazingly shallow water. If you child is playing in someone else's garden with a pond, keep a constant eye on him.

Pets

Small children are quite fearless and will want to stroke any dog, cat or other interesting-looking creature. Nine times out of ten this is perfectly safe, but the tenth time can give a baby a very nasty and unnerving, if not actually dangerous, experience. If it is your own pet which you can trust there is no problem. But beware of other people's pets, especially if they are not used to small children. Even a hamster can give a nasty bite.

When your baby is very small and you want to leave him outside for his rest, a cat-net should be used — just in case. They can be bought at baby shops.

Doors

Slamming doors is a favourite game. You can open, slam. Open, slam. Endless fun, even if Mother and the neighbours need earplugs. But a warning — this is not a game for two. If a little friend wants to join in this game, distract them both with something more exciting. Two small children can have a great time with a big grocery box.

Visiting

This can be fun, or a nightmare. Warn your friends that your baby is at the age when he gets at everything and that it would be unwise to leave the best china around. Tactfully remove some of the more obvious hazards yourself. If you have a car it is a good idea to carry a collapsible fireguard in the boot. A portable chair or pram straps that can be fixed to an ordinary kitchen chair can take the trauma out of eating away from home.

Harness and reins

As soon as your baby can sit upright, invest in a harness so that he cannot pull himself out of his pram or — as can all too easily happen — so that he cannot crawl to the other end and unbalance the pram so that it tips up. He will need strapping into his high chair too. By this time he will have graduated from a cradle to a drop-sided cot and falling out of bed ceases to be a problem.

When he begins to walk he will not want to hold your hand because his hands are much too useful for touching things, picking things up and generally waving about. Use reins if you are out shopping and he wants to get out of his pushchair. It slows things up considerably — he is not very fast on his feet yet and there is an infinity of fascinating sights and sounds worth stopping for — but letting him walk is highly rewarding and instructive. This book is about encouraging your child's curiosity so that he finds out about the world and builds up a wide vocabulary, but unless you are sure that he is safe you cannot leave him to explore. This is why we have spent some time on safety: for your peace of mind and for his benefit.

Things a crawling and standing baby needs and does

Sight

Your child is learning very fast now and the more he learns the more he wants and needs to learn. He will want a wheeled toy on a piece of string so that he can pull it towards him and work out why it comes. He will experiment with hiding things and gradually discover that hidden things do not disappear. He will want to explore and examine everything he sees. He will get into low cupboards and big boxes and underneath things.

You can begin showing him picture books on your knee, preferably board books with simple coloured pictures. Getting out and about in his pram is enjoyable and he will look around him and see what is going on with great interest. He will sit happily in the trolley at the supermarket. You can now safely leave him outside for his rest time, safely strapped in but with a few toys to play with.

Check his toybox and throw out any broken toys. Add to the geometric shapes described in Chapter 3. Get him some bright plastic nesting cups or boxes — they are good for putting things in and taking them out again.

Sound

He will be even more interested in sounds and what makes them and will crawl towards a strange new sound to see what makes it. Keep your record player out of reach, however.

He will also be making sounds himself — banging things, rattling things, ringing things. And, of course, he will begin to sing, giving his voice a test run.

He will enjoy being sung to and adore the finger play and tickling games described in the previous chapter.

Try hard not to use baby talk — he will get plenty of that from friends and relatives. If you talk to him properly his speech will progress a great deal more quickly.

Touch

He will be getting into everything so he will begin to discover for himself how different things feel. Gardens are wonderful places for him at this stage — there are so many shapes, colours and textures; things to break, crush and tear; the stones are heavy and cold; the grass rustles; the path is rough to crawl on — a profusion of sense impressions it is impossible to sort out.

Add to his toys things with different textures. A wooden block covered in sandpaper makes an interesting addition.

Smell

Now he is beginning to come across a whole new range of smells as he crawls around the house and garden. To this extent you can let him educate himself, by finding out about plants and flour smells, earth smells, the smell of hot stone in the sunshine, of furniture polish and carpet dust, the cat and the shoe cupboard. You can help him along by letting him experience the things that you handle that have their own particular smell — parsley, oranges, washing-up liquid, soap.

Taste

It is now much less trouble to feed him on food you know he likes: by this time he will have made his preferences clear. Even so, vary his diet by introducing new baby foods to him every now and then. His memory is short: food he rejected decisively three months ago may be happily accepted today.

By now he will be sitting in his high chair and joining the family for meals. He can certainly start tasting the food the rest of you are eating; it is good for him and makes him very much one of you. In our own home the new baby always had the first spoonful of the delicious gravy that ran from the Sunday joint when it was carved.

A sieve or liquidizer is very good for mincing his food quickly. It gives a more interesting texture than that of most proprietary brand baby foods.

Physical

His body is now a really useful tool in the business of satisfying his insatiable curiosity. It takes him where the interesting sight or sound is and allows him to discover all about it. Objects that were once too high for him to get at can be reached by pulling himself upright.

When he does stand up like this he is learning to master a new, important physical skill: to balance on two legs. Once he has become proficient at pulling himself up, you will soon notice another advance: he will let go of the table-leg or whatever support he pulled himself up by to examine the treasure he has found with both hands. At first he will usually quietly subside onto his bottom on the floor, but after a while he will be able to balance himself for some time. His first steps will be experimental and very tottery and for some time after these experiments have started crawling will still be his normal way of getting about. If he sees something interesting while he is learning to walk he will drop to his hands and knees immediately and scuttle over to it.

Crawling upstairs is something he has to learn sooner or later: be sure he does it under your supervision. In fact, going up is not too bad: it is coming down that is the problem. At first he will be very hesitant, but he will finally learn the contour of your own particular staircase and negotiate it at what appears to be breakneck speed.

His hands at this stage have become more flexible and sensitive. He can pick up an object with his fingers and thumb although he cannot yet let it go until he sees something else he likes better. He will use his index finger to poke at things.

Your baby will love being lifted into the air (not too roughly) by his father, and riding on his knee.

Social

Your baby is now becoming a sociable and responsive member of your family. He will wave bye-bye, play 'clap hands' and adore 'peep-bo' — he is beginning to understand that even when something is out of sight it still exists. He may hide a toy in a box and 'discover' it again with great excitement and satisfaction and he will do this over and over again until he is satisfied that it really does stay there once he has put it there.

He will love to give you things or, at least, to pretend to give them to you, because he has not yet learned how to let go. He will laugh at a surprising sound or a funny face and scream with laughter when you 'drop' him at the end of a bouncing game. Interestingly, he will repeat something that makes you laugh.

At this time he will often show fear of strangers. This is not a sign that he is becoming anti-social. On the contrary, it represents a big step towards his maturity because it shows that he is able to distinguish between known and unknown faces.

He begins to understand commands like 'No!' 'Come here' and 'Give it to Daddy.' Mother is still very much the centre of his universe; he needs constant physical contact with her and when he is not actually touching her he likes to keep her in sight.

Practical suggestions

Sight

Nesting cups

This is a cheap, sturdy and extremely versatile toy. It consists of a series of brightly coloured cups of graded sizes which fit into each other and can be built into a tower.

They will be used for innumerable other games — for putting things into, for rattling things in, for hiding things under, for drinking from, as a digging tool in the sandpit, and in other games he will discover for himself. The cups will last for years and he can begin to play with them now. Do not expect him to fit them together or pile them in order — yet. But they will be ready for him when he can. Buy him round cups because he will not be able to manipulate square cups at this stage.

Peg Toys

These are small wheeled toys that can be pulled along on a string. Little fat figures fit into holes in trucks, cars, ships, aircraft, etc. The dolls will be played with separately later in imaginative games, but at this stage of his development your baby will be content to try to put them in and take them out of their holes.

Peg Toys

Saucepans

Your saucepan cupboard is a treasure trove — let him make full use of it. Be sure, of course, that there is nothing dangerous there. He will love the saucepans and the noise he can make with them, and you can increase the fun by putting a few unexpected extras in — a wooden spoon, plastic pastry cutters, the egg whisk, etc.

Rag doll

Rag dolls are pretty cheap but you can easily make one yourself. He will soon begin to regard it as some kind of real person and will continually put it into real-life situations — in bed, in a chair, trying to feed it, etc.

Rag doll

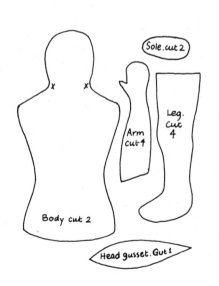

Cut the pieces out in strong cotton material or use felt. Use kapok or nylon for stuffing.

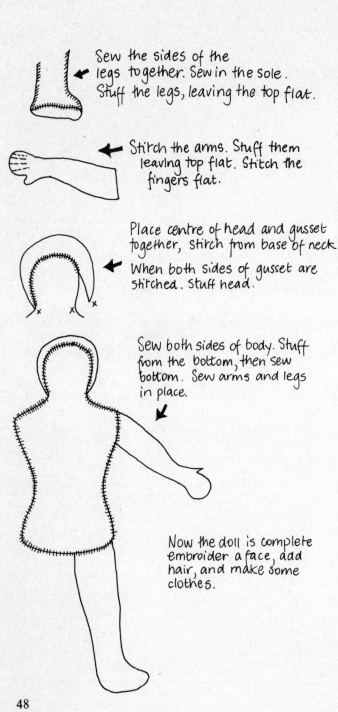

Sew the sides of the legs together. Sew in the sole. Stuff the legs, leaving the top flat.

Stitch the arms. Stuff them leaving top flat. Stitch the fingers flat.

Place centre of head and gusset together, stitch from base of neck

When both sides of gusset are stitched. Stuff head.

Sew both sides of body. Stuff from the bottom, then sew bottom. Sew arms and legs in place.

Now the doll is complete embroider a face, add hair, and make some clothes.

To make hair for the doll wind wool round a piece of card

length you want hair to be

cut

Stitch hair to a piece of tape and stirch onto doll. You can plait it, bunch it or leave it loose.

Bubbles

Blow bubbles for him. Bubble-blowing kits are cheap, but do-it-your-self is even cheaper. All you need is a piece of wire bent into a ring with a handle and some washing-up liquid.

He will watch the bubbles float and occasionally try to catch them. Play this game for a short time only and then put it away for another day.

Cardboard boxes

A cardboard box of any size is a potential toy. So before you throw away that cereal or egg-box let your baby investigate it. Let him pull out the lining paper and crumple it with his fingers and take it to his mouth to see what it tastes like. Let him discover the few bits of cereal at the bottom. When he has had his fun you can throw the box away.

Don't forget that at this age the wrapping round a parcel is just as interesting to a child as the contents. He is too young to appreciate building blocks but cardboard cartons can be stuffed with newspaper and sealed with sticky tape for him to carry about.

Books

You can start showing him books with simple illustrations. He cannot manage flimsy pages himself at this stage, so board or rag books are the only sensible answer. At first he will try to pick up the pictures, but he will soon learn that these are not real. After a while he will enjoy helping you to turn each page to the familiar but always exciting picture overleaf.

Sound

Drum

A biscuit-tin and wooden-spoon drum makes a splendid noise but it can be distinctly wearing after the first five minutes. A more attractive — and quieter — model can easily be made. You need a large can (something like a seven-pint beer can) with the ends cut off, a piece of rubber or strong plastic and some strong cord.

Cut two circles of rubber about an inch bigger in diameter than the can. Make twelve holes about half an inch from the circumference of each rubber disc and thread these with the cords to cover the ends of the can. This will be quieter for you and more interesting for your baby.

Nursery rhymes

These are among the finest of all ways of advancing your baby's education as generations of mothers have discovered. Sing them to him over and over again — he will love the repetition and they will provide the very first words he will use. He will pick up rhythm, rhyme and sentence construction from them.

Gramophone record

A useful aid to nursery rhymes sung by you is a nursery-rhyme gramophone record. You can sing with it and he will soon learn to recognize the rhymes. It also has the effect of making him aware that the rhymes exist outside himself and you.

Knee riding

In these traditional games the baby is bounced on an adult's leg to the varying rhythms demanded by the rhyme. A traditional rhyme with very attractive words is:

> A farmer went trotting upon his grey mare
> Bumpety bumpety bump
> With his daughter behind him so rosy and fair
> Bumpety bumpety bump
>
> A magpie cried 'caw' and they all tumbled down
> Bumpety bumpety bump
> The mare broke her knees and the farmer his crown
> Bumpety bumpety bump
>
> The mischievous magpie flew laughing away
> Bumpety bumpety bump
> And vowed he would serve them the same the next day
> Bumpety bumpety bump

Perhaps the best known of all is:

> Ride-a-cock horse to Banbury Cross
> To see a fine lady upon a white horse;
> Rings on her fingers and bells on her toes
> She shall have music wherever she goes.

And here is a lovely Geordie dandling rhyme:

> Dance for your daddy
> My little laddie
> Dance for your daddy
> My little lamb
> You shall have a fishy

51

On a little dishy
You shall have a fishy
When the boat comes in.

In this one your baby is not bounced on your lap but held so that he can flex his legs on your lap.

For the next one you cross your legs and sit your baby on your ankle, holding his hands. On the word 'Hup!' you uncross your leg, swinging the baby over and setting him gently on the floor. Once he gets to know this game, a dramatic pause before the 'Hup!' is much appreciated.

A man and his dog they went to Dover
Came to a stile and ... Hup! they went over.

Finally another old favourite. For this you sit the baby on your lap facing you and hold his hands. The first two lines are spoken very seriously and intently to enhance the drama. He will soon begin to enjoy this. On the word 'fall' you open your legs and let the baby slip down between them, holding him firmly the while. He is then pulled back onto your lap and cheerfully bounced for the last two lines:

Humpty Dumpty sat on a wall,
Humpty Dumpty had a great ... fall!!
All the king's horses
And all the king's men
Couldn't put Humpty together again.

Touch

Finger painting with food
Don't worry if your baby puts his fingers into his food and spreads it over his tray. He is doing a kind of primitive painting and enjoying the whole sensation of making patterns and shapes of his own. It feels good to him so let him get the feeling of a little granulated sugar or some large cake crumbs. He can touch and eat at the same time.

Different places to crawl
He will discover the texture of the ground by crawling over it and experiencing it directly with his hands and knees. Difference in sur-

face texture is something that you completely forget about if you wear shoes. But your baby will know what lino, matting, carpet, tile, parquet, grass and concrete feel like.

Sandpaper brick
Cover a block of wood with sandpaper and leave another one of the same size quite smooth. The difference in texture will both interest him and educate his fingers in sensitivity. You can cover another one with velvet or corduroy.

Touch book
Your baby will now begin to enjoy sitting on your lap and sharing a book with you. Apart from the simple picture book described earlier a 'touch' book is great fun, helps your baby to refine his sense of touch and is very easy to make.

Take a number of six-inch square pieces of cardboard and cover each side with a different textured material — fabric, polystyrene, cellophane, moulded wallpaper, corduroy, satin, tinfoil, etc. Fix the pages together with string or ring clips and you have your baby's first touch book. You can, of course, add to it from time to time when you come across a new and interesting texture.

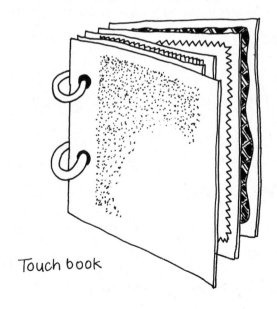

Touch book

Smell

Containers
Save the empty containers that have retained the smell of their contents — dessert cartons, tobacco tins, curry and spice tins, talc shakers, etc. — and let him play with them and smell them.

Food
Let him smell the difference between the various dishes you feed him with before you let him actually taste them — fish, tomato soup, yoghurt, chocolate pudding. In this way he will learn to associate a particular smell with a particular food and to anticipate it.

Taste

His food
His first attempts to feed himself will be made at this stage of his development and so this is a good time, again, to introduce new tastes. He will be so absorbed in trying to master this new art and to manipulate his first tool that you can introduce new foods and flavours without his really noticing. The texture of his food is every bit as important to him as the taste, so present him with changes of texture as well as of flavour.

Your food
Now that he is mobile he will find many new and curious things to taste. See that they are all palatable and harmless. Let him join you when you are cooking and allow him to taste with you — the raw cake mixture, the sliced carrot, the glacé cherry. Don't forget that he will soon be standing on a chair helping you.

Physical

Boxes

Big boxes are godsends. Make tunnels out of grocery boxes by cutting the ends off so that he can crawl through.

Boxes as boxes, of course, are a constant source of joy and interest. He will get into one and sit there, then he will get out. He will learn how to climb over the side, to turn the box in all directions to use it as he wants.

Boxes

Bridge

Bridge

Place a smooth wide plank across two low piles of books so that he can crawl across. He will tend to turn round and crawl back again and go on doing this repeatedly. It is good for his sense of balance and his spatial sense.

Rough-house

He will begin to enjoy a romp with his father, climbing on to him, pulling his nose and exploring his features. He will also enjoy strenuous fun, wriggling and kicking and being thrown in the air and caught again (but not too high — a fear of falling is built into all human beings). Knee games and lap rides with Daddy are always very acceptable.

'More'

If after any pleasurable physical activity you say 'More?' in a questioning manner and then repeat whatever he has enjoyed he will very quickly associate the word with the actions and start to use it himself.

Sunday morning

Sunday morning can become the time when he comes into bed with his parents for all kinds of wonderful games and romps. He can crawl into the depths of the bed or climb the mountain of his daddy's knees only to have them collapse time and time again in a most exciting fashion. Most parents will find the invention of Sunday morning games an easy matter . . . and they only end when you are exhausted!

Baby Walker

This is a solid, four-wheeled cart with a raised handle at one end just the right height for your baby to hold when he is standing. He can push it along easily, but it is heavy enough not to tip up and is thus most useful in learning to walk.

Although he will not be taking his first steps just yet, it is useful to get him acquainted with a baby walker. It is, moreover, a toy he will go on using for years after it has fulfilled its original purpose.

Baby walker

Social

Your baby is now beginning to take a positive role in his social activities and there are many well-established ways of helping him to do this.

Action Songs

These are lap games where you sing a song and you and your baby clap either your own hands or each other's. There are no rules to these games and you can introduce as many variations and adaptations as you think fit.

> Clap handies, clap handies
> Till daddy comes home
> 'Cause daddy has pennies
> And mummy has none.

> Pat-a-cake, pat-a-cake, baker's man
> Bake me a cake as fast as you can;
> Prick it and pat it and mark it with 'B' [or baby's initial]
> Put it in the oven for baby and me.

Peep-bo

This will continue to be a favourite game

Talk to your baby

At some time during this crawling and standing stage, your baby will probably acquire his first few words — 'Mum-mum' 'Dad-dad' — but, of course, he can understand a great many more. So ask him to do simple things: point to the ball and say 'Give me the ball!' Point to the door and say 'Shut the door!' 'Where are Johnny's eyes?' 'Where are Mummy's eyes?' 'Where are your fingers?' Your pleasure in his correct response is an enormous stimulus to greater efforts on his part.

5 Toddling and Walking

By the time your baby is eighteen months old he will almost certainly have mastered the art of balance and be able to walk quite confidently. His ability to walk is achieved surprisingly quickly once he has nerved himself to let go of the chair or whatever it is that is supporting him and to launch himself across the room. Your encouragement and pleasure at his courage will make him want to repeat the experiment. Mothers seem to know how to do this instinctively and one of the most common and charming babyhood scenes in every country in the world is the mother bending and holding out her arms to the infant tottering towards her. In the early days of walking he will still find it quicker to crawl expertly towards anything he is really interested in but he soon discards this method of travel for his own two feet.

It is now that he begins to follow you round the house 'helping', which inevitably means getting under your feet. It is less frustrating for you both if you turn his inexhaustible energy to some semi-practical use. Let him carry something round for you and let him join in what you are doing as much as possible. Small children love helping to make the bed and this can be even more fun if a bit of a romp is involved, with him diving in and out of a heap of rumpled bedclothes.

He will be delighted to pick up shoes and toys from the floor and this in itself gives rise to a whole new set of problems. Can he bend down without actually falling over? Once he has picked up the toy, where does he put it? Are there any more where that one came from? Can my mummy see how clever I am? Children at this age never tire of solving problems and quite suddenly the world is full of problems.

All his skills will be improving rapidly now, and relatives and friends who miss seeing him for a month will notice big changes taking place during that time. He will, for instance, like to carry bulky objects about and will try to move things far beyond the limits of his strength. Then he will work out what is possible and what is impossible and another step forward will have been taken. His urge to explore and find out is irrepressible.

Being able to walk opens up new territories to his inquisitiveness. With his greatly improved balance he will climb up onto furniture to get at things beyond his reach and this in itself will reveal to him new and unseen vistas, new and even more interesting objects to grab at. He will also work out that if he wants to get something he can fetch something to climb onto. Another big step is the formation of his logical thought mechanisms, in his understanding of cause and effect.

Baby-proofing a room now becomes a bad dream, and most parents begin to realize that they can have a clean and tidy house or a happy baby, but not both.

New explorations at this age will certainly take your baby upstairs. This is a fraught moment for mothers. The toddler reaches the top step and wobbles dangerously, sublimely unaware of the abyss behind him and only intent on what lies ahead. In fact children of this age very rarely fall downstairs and even more rarely do themselves any more harm than to frighten themselves. Keep the child-proof gate fastened unless you are there to supervise mountaineering expeditions. The reason for this is not the danger of the stairs themselves, but the hidden mysteries of the upstairs or downstairs rooms.

Shopping expeditions take on a new and exciting aspect. Indeed, any outing is now a great adventure to be looked forward to. Do not forget that to you and your child these trips are quite different things. You cannot explain to him that you cannot stop at every notice, leaf, dog or wall that you pass. Equally, he cannot explain to you his passionate interest in all these things. There is no solution to this dilemma. A partial answer is to put him in the pushchair or supermarket trolley and give him something interesting to hold, and to compromise by taking ten minutes of the expedition at his pace. His great interest will probably arouse your own as well.

You will now begin to find that he becomes totally absorbed in any activity he undertakes and that his span of attention has noticeably increased. So has control of his body: his coordination of limb and eye is now very good. He will get extremely angry and frustrated if he has to change from one activity to another. Typical examples of this are, for instance, when he is dipping in the mud with an old spoon and it is time for his lunch, or when he is happily toddling along the pavement and you sweep him into his pushchair because you are in a hurry. His anger will be shortlived at this stage because some new activity can quickly attract his attention, but it is no less real for that. Parents generally learn that when he is cross he is easily distracted by some pleasurable activity — after all, he does like his dinner, he knows what 'bath' means, and the previous enjoyment is soon forgotten.

As his language expands he will be able to understand explanations. If he is playing with something fragile or dangerous, it is always better to give him a more attractive alternative than to try and take the object away from him. This again could easily be an occasion when he would react angrily because he very reasonably would not understand why the object has been removed.

He should begin to have bowel control and be able to use his pot. But don't fret if he still soils his nappies from time to time. If you ever get angry with him in these circumstances you may frighten him before he has real control of his bowels and he may conclude that it was not the accident but the faeces themselves that made you cross. This can lead to his withholding them and start all sorts of digestive and emotional troubles.

For parents this stage of their child's development is especially enthralling. He is desperately anxious to communicate, he will repeat words that you say over and over again and he will also put two words together himself and repeat these endlessly: 'See Daddy', 'See Paul', 'Mummy chair', 'More milk'. He will almost certainly begin to ask you to name things for him, pointing to them and saying 'Wass at?' just to hear you say the words. He will often reverse this procedure, pointing to things and naming them himself, so as to see your pleasure when he gets it right. Plainly he understands a great deal of what you are saying to him.

Now is the time when picture books become really important. He can have a special story-time on your knee before he goes to bed and he will adore his favourite book with its beloved sequences of familiar pictures. At this stage he will not be able to follow a story-line: that comes later when he will insist that you use exactly the same words in the same order and will correct you fiercely if you stray from the path of pure orthodoxy. At this stage a series of pictures with comments like 'Look at that pretty flower', 'That's a big horse', 'Isn't he a funny man, he's a clown' — are perfectly adequate.

60

Things a toddler needs and does

Sight

He is finding out quickly that everything has a name and is beginning to distinguish between one category and another. He will know which is his own mug — and that it looks different from all the other family mugs. He will begin to learn that not all four-legged animals are dogs: that small animals of a certain shape are called cats and big animals of another shape are called horses. He is learning by seeing that some things match and others don't, that there are incongruities around him (he will go on learning this for the rest of his life).

Sound

His hearing is getting more selective and he can distinguish the voices of his family even when he cannot see them. He is so busy with his eyes and his hands that his hearing can mark time if you are not careful to give him really quiet rest periods. Then he can pick out sounds individually as distinct from hearing them merged in a general household background noise — the singing of a bird, the rumble of a passing lorry, your own voice as you sing, the other children coming home from school.

He will love being sung to and his favourite little rhymes and songs will be established, even if he cannot yet join in and sing them.

Touch

With his greatly increased co-ordination he will be experimenting quite dramatically and wanting to test everything for its feel and texture. He will want to climb up to help you wash up, to feel the hot water and the cold, the bubbles, the washing-up liquid, the cutlery, the scouring brush, the steel wool. He will be happy digging with a spoon and a stick in the earth or sand although he is still too young to fill up pots and buckets; he will love the feel of what he is playing with, whether it is sand, mud, flour or earth.

Helping you cook will be great fun because it is now associated with nice tastes. He will feel the texture of pastry and put his finger on currants to know what they feel like. If he happens to reach this age when there is snow and ice about, he is extra lucky. These are a great wonder and he will play with them until he is blue (do not let this happen: a mutual ten-minute romp is enough for him and probably for you too). In autumn he will like the crackle of dry leaves and the noise and sensation of trampling through them. In summer he will like to walk through sand and, if his hands are held by an encouraging adult, he will love the sensation of the sea sliding over his toes. If he is well wrapped up he will like going out in the rain at any time of the year, splashing through puddles in his wellingtons and feeling the rain on his face.

By the time he goes to school he will have begun to understand the cycle of the weeks, the seasons and the year. At this earlier stage he will merely understand that some days are different from others.

Smell

He will now eagerly imitate your sniffing if you smell something and put it under his nose for his own sampling (it is much easier to sniff in than to blow down your nose, which is why little noses have to be constantly wiped). So let him smell anything interesting you happen to be handling, from your perfume to vinegar.

A slow trip round a flower-bed is useful, too. Park attendants are universally indulgent to small children who want to smell their beautiful flowers.

Now that he is helping in the kitchen he will be smelling things and taking much more notice than before: his earlier experiments are beginning to pay off.

Taste

He will become more choosey about his food and you should continue to offer him as wide a variety as possible while retaining his favourites. While helping you to cook or when you go shopping there will be a number of opportunities for him to taste new things: help him. If, for instance, he tastes the raw cake mixture and the cooked cake he will begin to understand the process of cooking. The same goes for vegetables and fruit.

Physical

The big step involved here is, literally, the big step — the first unaided step that he takes. This means that he has attained enough of a sense of balance to be confident of using it and, once this confidence has been reinforced by his own experience and your evident approval, he will want to practise this new skill at every opportunity. This can be inconvenient when you are in a hurry to get home, but the urge is extremely strong and his annoyance when it is frustrated is understandable.

At the same time he is developing his manipulative skills. He will use his index finger to poke at things and to prise things out. He will begin to turn knobs and twist screws. He will drink from a cup unaided, holding it with two hands. He will pull a toy on a string behind him as he walks. At first this will present the problem of divided attention because he will want to look at it at the same time and he will frequently fall over trying to do both at once. Eventually he will accept that the toy will still be there at the end of the journey and he will have mastered this problem of balance.

His clothes begin to mean something to him too. He associates them with the right parts of his body and makes conscious — if not very successful — efforts to put his feet into his shoes and his gloves on his hands.

Social

He will still want to be with you or near you for nearly all his waking hours, but will cheerfully accept another adult he knows well or has seen often enough to get used to. He does not take much notice of other children yet when he plays, but he may follow them if they move away, showing that he has been aware of their presence. He now enjoys a conversation, even if his only contribution is 'No!'

Practical suggestions

Sight

Pictures
Take a fresh look at the pictures round his room or the place where he sleeps. They should be pictures of things he can recognize — big, bold, colourful and without too much detail. A good way of finding suitable pictures is to cut them out of magazines. Mount them carefully on paper (brown wrapping paper will do) and then stick to the wall with Sellotape, drawing pins or, if you are worried about your wallpaper, with Plastitac, a kind of adhesive plasticine which sticks firmly but comes off cleanly leaving no mark on the wallpaper.

Picture cards
When you change the pictures in his room, do not throw the old ones away. Remount them (cut them out again if you can't unstick them) on cards about 6″ x 8″ in size — the fronts and backs of cereal packets are ideal, as are the stiffening cards found in new shirts. Stick a picture on each side of these home-made cards and let your baby handle them. He will turn them over and over again, getting great pleasure out of seeing his favourite familiar pictures. The new pictures on his wall will, of course, end up the same way.

Crayons
He can start using crayons. Buy the thick wax ones, not the small thin ones. Most stationers and art shops stock them. Give him a good-sized sheet of white paper — an opened-out paper bag will do — and let him see you make a mark on it. Then show him how to do it by putting a crayon in his hand and marking the paper with it. At this pre-scribbling stage he will only make random marks and lines, but he is not too young to see what he is doing.

Steamed-up windows
He has already achieved a number of finger-paintings by spreading his food about in interesting ways. If you hold him by a steamed-up window and show him how to do it, he can make more finger-paintings. And the cold, wet feel of this activity will interest him too.

Cutlery box

He is still too young to sort things but he will enjoy handling the cutlery and will take it out of its box, turn it over in his hands and then replace each piece in one of the partitions. He will also enjoy the noise it makes. Make sure there is nothing sharp or pointed.

Bricks

It is worth looking out for bricks for him and, of course, they are easily made. They should be of a regular size so that they stack easily on each other, i.e., if the basic cube is 2" x 2" x 2" the other bricks should all be multiples of 2" x 2" x 2" x 4" or 2" x 2" x 8".

Use hard wood and smooth it well and if you paint the bricks make sure you use lead-free paint. But most people find that there are good bricks on sale cheaply enough to make do-it-yourself bricks hardly worth while.

A posting-box

You can make him his first posting-box out of any cardboard box which has a lid (a shoe box is ideal). Cut a round hole of about one and a half inches in the lid. Give him lots of things he can post in the box — corks, milk bottle tops, conkers, pieces of coloured card, bricks — anything that is handy and of the right size.

Posting box

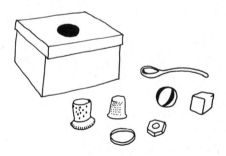

Colour and shape

Add to his collection of coloured wooden shapes. This time cut them a size larger and in two different thicknesses. Stick to three or four basic lead-free colours so that each shape is painted in a different colour which is repeated in each different thickness.

Sound

Almost all wheeled toys make some satisfactory sort of noise, but you can always add some kind of extra noise-making device if you do not consider it enough — rattling tin lids, aluminium foil, yoghurt pots or something easily improvised. Some wheeled toys have elaborate noise-making machinery — ringing bells, automatic trip hammers and the like: however these can be nerve-racking.

Attach a big bead or cotton reel to the end of the string so that the toy can be pulled along more easily.

Wooden xylophone

At this stage he will enjoy banging a xylophone. Wooden ones are the best: they look, sound and feel better and are generally stronger than anything else. They are easy to make from different lengths of any really hard wood, loosely nailed across two battens. Let him bang it with a wooden stick. Or you can make a professional drumstick by stuffing a piece of chamois leather tightly with cottonwool and tying it very firmly over the end of the stick.

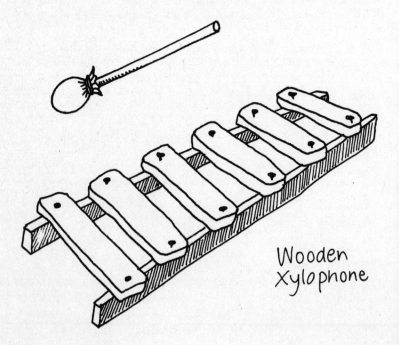

Wooden
Xylophone

Nursery rhyme and folksong records

Introduce him to a few suitable records. Listen to them with him and sing the songs as they are played. You will find that he is already showing a preference for certain songs, usually those with a strong beat. Show him the brightly coloured record sleeves too — he will soon learn to recognize them and to associate them with the sounds he likes.

More songs to sing together

A favourite lullaby: 'Twinkle, twinkle little star'.
A favourite nursery rhyme: 'Baa-baa black sheep'.
A favourite finger-play:

> Insky-winsky spider, climbed up the spout
> Down came the rain and washed the spider out.
>
> Out came the sun and dried up all the rain
> So insky-winsky spider climbed the spout again.

The actions that accompany this are very simple to perform but difficult to explain. Briefly, the thumbs and forefingers are placed together, thumbs against forefingers, and then the bottom pair released and brought round and above the upper pair, then the process is repeated. This climbing motion is carried over the first line. The second line is accompanied by a shimmering downward motion of the hands as the spider is washed out. On the third line the forearms are opened palms up, descriptive of the sun coming out, and the fourth line has the same movements as the first.

A favourite action song is 'Sing a song of sixpence' — and don't forget to peck your baby's nose on the last line.

Touch

Water play

He has been playing with water in his bath for a long time now and he has also stood on a chair and watched you wash up. (Even if you have a dishwasher there are always occasions when you actually wash things in the sink — awkwardly shaped saucepans, the grill tray, even washing out dishcloths). Let him wash up some things with you — a yoghurt cup under the tap, a saucepan in the suds, a pan with a bristly brush. He will notice the different temperatures and textures, the slipperiness of the suds, the soddenness of the wet cloth, the coldness of the drips from the cold tap. To you it is all a chore: to him it is a feast of sights, sounds and sensations.

Another great game is 'helping' to wash the floor. He will soon learn that wet floorcloths hold a great deal of water and that if buckets are pulled over the water goes absolutely everywhere! But under supervision it is a lovely messy game for him to play. He can even be useful sometimes because he will love mopping up puddles with a cloth.

Earth and mud

He is bound to get very dirty playing with these glorious materials so get used to the idea now and have enough cheap, tough coveralls to cope with the situation. He will use his hands and fingers, but will like to have a spoon or stick to dig with.

Often by accident he will discover that earth plus water equals mud, a highly desirable substance with a fascinating consistency. Do not discourage him. On the other hand if he is dressed in his best clothes do not expect him to realize this. There seems to be a rule that all parents find this out the hard way — once!

Humpty Dumpty

Make him a big Humpty Dumpty out of scraps of material. Make it about two feet high and a foot across and choose all sorts of fabrics with different textures — e.g., a satin face, corduroy body, fur fabric hair, hessian arms.

Humpty Dumpty

make him out of different textured materials

68

Smell

Out-of-door smells
Take him into the various shops you visit — don't just leave him sitting outside in his pram. Baker, greengrocer, fishmonger, hardware shop, bank — each has its own unique smell.

Expeditions round the garden or into the park or into the country proper have their own range of smells — leaves, flowers, sticks, animals, buildings.

Bathroom
Make a game of smelling all the pots and creams. He will recognize his own baby powder — but how about Daddy's aftershave, or your shampoo?

Kitchen
If he is actively 'helping' you when you work in the kitchen he should have plenty of opportunity to use his nose to smell spices, sweet things, soup, pastry baking, fruit cooking and many other things. Make sure he does have these opportunities.

Taste

Crumbs
Crumbs of various kinds are harmless and tasty and will often be painstakingly picked up and sampled. So if you leave a few cake or biscuit crumbs (not stale ones) in the bottom of the tin or packet, don't throw them away, let your baby have them. Incidentally, picking up little crumbs is good practice for his hand and eye co-ordination.

Cooking
As before, let him taste the things you are cooking. If he is helping to put in the flour, the sugar or the raisins he will naturally want to taste them and the mixture that results from them. And don't forget that there are other throwaway tastes as well — the long string of apple peel, the crisped bacon rind, the squeezed lemon.

Shopping

While you are shopping, open up a harmless packet or two that you have bought so that he can sample your goodies. He will want to break little flakes off the crusty loaf and chew the corner of your jelly cubes, but you don't mind and the family need not know!

Physical

Climbing

If, as described previously, you make a bridge a few inches high by placing a smooth plank across a couple of blocks or piles of books, he will crawl onto them and balance proudly. This is good for his self-confidence.

Big engine

At this stage of his development, a big wheeled toy — train, truck or bus — is good for him. He can sit on it so that his feet touch the ground either side and push himself along. The wooden ones are the most attractive but the plastic ones are cheaper and he will not notice the difference. A wooden one is not too difficult to make, and once made it will serve generations of children.

Rocker

A small chair on rockers is always popular and will be gratefully used especially when he is tired. He will then rock himself comfortably and quietly until someone notices that he is ready for a cuddle and a proper rest.

Fit-together train

He will like playing with a wooden train that pegs together simply so that he can pull it along. Large bricks that fit together are good for him to push along — he will have more control over them because they have no wheels.

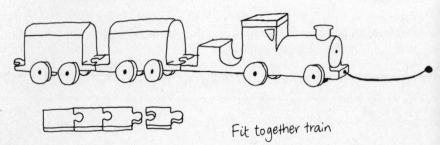

Fit together train

Hammering

A hammering toy with wooden pegs that can be bashed with a wooden hammer is good at this age. As he gains in skill he will bang more accurately and work out that when all the pegs have been banged through, the toy can be turned over and the pegs hammered back again.

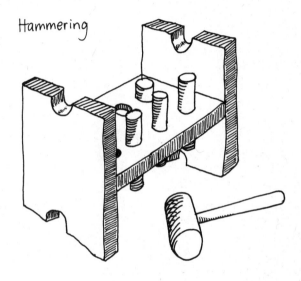

Hammering

Clothes pegs

Paint some clothes-pegs with bright lead-free paint and let him clip them to the sides of a tin box. You can paint each side of the tin a different colour to match the pegs. He may not notice the colours at first but let him discover them for himself. Store the pegs in the tin when you put it away.

Social

Finger puppets

These can be made by cutting the fingers off a pair of gloves and decorating them with bits of wool or felt or a felt-tipped pen to make little people.

Finger puppets

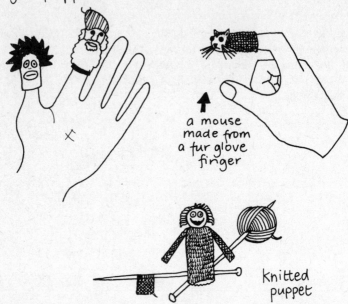

a mouse
made from
a fur glove
finger

knitted
puppet

You can tell all sorts of stories with finger puppets, hide them, change them, use them on both hands. You can even let your baby pull them off and try to put them on his own small fingers. A little later you can leave him with them and he will play with them and rehearse old stories or make up new ones for himself.

The best finger puppets are knitted from oddments of wool and can be made very quickly.

Use size 10 or 11 needles. Work in stocking stitch.
Cast on 16 stitches; knit length of your middle finger.
Change colour for face — knit 1 inch.
K.2 tog. along line 8 times. Purl back.
K.2 tog. along line 4 times.
Thread through last four stitches, and slip-stitch to make
    glove finger.
Arms: cast on 4 stitches. Knit for 1½ inches.
Stuff head with cotton wool and run thread round
    neck.

You can decorate this little puppet with any bits of trimming and make any individual characters.

Two little dicky birds

All you need for this game are two little bits of sticky paper, one on each index finger. When Peter and Paul fly away the index finger is tucked into the palm and the middle finger shown to your baby. When Peter and Paul come back the index finger is rediscovered with the bit of paper on it. This is endless fun and real magic: many seven-year-olds still have not solved this mystery.

> Two little dicky birds
> Sitting on a wall
> One named Peter, one named Paul.
> Fly away Peter,
> Fly away Paul.
> Come back Peter,
> Come back Paul.

Tommy Thumb

You can dress you fingers up with finger puppets if you like but this game is just as much fun without.

> Tommy Thumb, Tommy Thumb
> Where are you?
> Here I am, here I am
> How do you do?

> Peter Pointer, Peter Pointer etc. (Index finger)
> Toby Tall, Toby Tall etc. (middle finger)
> Ruby Ring, Ruby Ring etc (ring finger)
> Baby Small, Baby Small etc. (little finger)
> Fingers All, Fingers All etc. (all fingers)

Hide your hands behind your back and produce them with the relevant finger on show. When you reach 'How do you do' they are suitably waggled.

Talking

Talk to your baby. Involve and interest him in what you are doing. He will learn sounds quite naturally as you point things out to him. Remember to use adjectives and make him aware of what they mean — light, heavy, hot, cold, big, small, and so on. Adverbs like up, down, in, out, now, etc., will gradually take on more meaning.

6 Talking to the Family

There is not necessarily any correlation between physical development and the ability to talk and, if it is any consolation to parents worried about a taciturn infant, both Albert Einstein and the Duke of Wellington were late talkers. A child will talk when it is ready to talk and any attempts to hasten the process are doomed to failure. The best encouragement you can give to your child is to talk to him, read to him, sing to him and ensure that he is exposed to the conversation of others. Provided that you are not hindering him by anticipating everything he wants so that he never has a chance to ask for it, nature will take its course. The only real exception to this is if your child's hearing is defective and this would almost certainly have revealed itself much earlier through his lack of response to noises: but if a parent thinks there is something wrong with a child's ears, an early visit to the doctor is essential.

Assuming that everything is normal, your child will begin to speak some time after he begins to toddle. That is to say, he will begin to put words together in short phrases rather than use single words. This means that he has mastered the fundamentals of language and is beginning to use it not only for demands but for comments, descriptions and statements. Even with a vocabulary limited to about two hundred words he will be able to make himself understood nearly all the time and he will be constantly practising and adding to the words he knows. By the time he is seven, he will have increased his vocabulary to more than five thousand words, a startling achievement.

At the time he is beginning to speak he will know a little about a great many things, but the little he does know he will know extremely well. Everything he has learned he will have tested over and over again. He will have copied other people, comparing and correcting his own actions and judging his own performance himself.

He can walk now, but is not so good at stopping suddenly. He can push a barrow in a straight line but it will tip over if he tries to turn a corner with it. He can push his feet into his shoes, but he cannot make them stay in. He can carry a cup of water, but finds it difficult to put it down without spilling some. The toy cars he is trying to fill his arms with will fall out before he can finish picking them all up. It can be very frustrating and you will find him howling with rage at times and fiercely unwilling to let you help him. The next chapter deals with the frustrations of the 'Terrible Twos' as they are often called. Basically, however, this is a time when he is revelling in the new sociability that he has discovered and he is not exclusively absorbed in the constant challenges by which he measures his achievements.

This is a wonderful time: he is beginning to imitate the things he sees going on around him and he will use the objects he finds in the way you use them. He'll pick up the broom, talk into the telephone, use your face cream, put sugar in the cups, milk in the cat's saucer — anything and everything that you do. In fact, when you can't see him you can be pretty sure that he is copying you doing something around the house. And it is really no use scolding him if he overdoes it; adults may be satisfied with a few sheets of toilet paper; he will certainly want to unroll the lot.

This sort of incident can happen many times a day. It can be both exasperating and wearing, but it is an essential process and is often very rewarding too. Every day will bring its new achievement — a new word, an improved skill, a longer venture into the garden. It is a great age for posting things too, so you will have to put yourself in your child's place if you find the car keys or the dog's collar missing. When our younger son was this age a purse was missing just when the milkman was due to be paid. It wasn't in any of the obvious places: wastepaper basket, under the sofa, down the loo, but inspiration on his mother's part ran it to earth in a saucepan in the pan cupboard — and in three minutes flat.

All these things he is doing suggest a new and wider range of toys — especially toys he can use to imitate you. A toy telephone, a miniature dustpan and brush, a doll and cradle — these are toys which will be played with for months to come. Add to them judiciously and not too often. Do not, for instance, allow him to be overwhelmed with dozens of new toys at Christmas or his birthday. He will literally not know which one to play with first. Far better to let him have the fun of opening them all (only a heart of stone could forbid him that!) and then put most of them away to be brought out as the occasion demands.

His speech at this time is so limited and quaint and his mispronunciation so wild that you may be tempted to meet him half-way by using his words and his pronunciation. This is unwise for obvious reasons. It is far better to speak properly, using the correct words. Then he can hear how words are pronounced and correct himself. Find a way of using the word properly, in a different and interesting context.

Do not forget that his own limited speech has to bear an enormous burden of meaning for him. He is quite unable to convey to you the complexity of his reactions — and they can be quite complex. For instance, at two years old our elder son saw a ten-year-old friend fall down and badly graze his knee. He was very impressed by this and clearly had an understanding of the pain and general inconvenience caused. For several days afterwards he would say 'Jick fall down' over and over again, sometimes catching hold of us and looking at us very intently. Obviously the incident meant a great deal more to him than he was able to convey in the three words he had available to describe it. A child two years older would not only be able to describe the incident quite lucidly but might also throw in an imaginary ambulance as a bonus.

Little outings and occurrences now have a special significance, especially if they are repeated. A ride on a bus, a trip to the park to feed the ducks, watching the postman empty the pillar-box, watching workmen dig a hole, a visit to a neighbour — all these have something the same and something different that can be talked about. He will be very interested in being talked to about them and talking back in his turn.

Life will become so very interesting and he will be so busy doing things that he will not notice that he is getting tired. Instead he will become more and more fractious. Make sure that bedtime is a regular routine, and that he never stays up beyond his proper time. He will often fight this (though not as hard as he will a little later on) but really be content to lose the battle. His final burst of energy will be in the bath, splashing and playing, and again, he will often put up a struggle to stay in. But if you remind him that you or Daddy has a bedtime story for him this will usually do the trick. Reassure him that he has your full attention and prepare him to go to sleep. Try very hard not to miss this last vital quarter of an hour. It is often very difficult, especially if you have a younger baby to look after. We solved the problem by getting a neighbour's schoolgirl daughter to cope with the new baby — she was delighted and flattered — for the vital minutes while the two-year-old was cuddled and tucked into bed.

Things your child needs at this stage

Sight

He will continue to enjoy trips outside and expeditions of all kinds, however short or mundane. They may mean little to you but they will give him a wealth of new and valuable experience. A walk with Daddy occasionally is a very exciting affair because he goes to different places, sees different things and uses different words.

He will begin to enjoy sorting things but will note their shapes rather than their colour — things go together because they are circular or square rather than because they are blue or red. He will want to post things in a posting-box and he may also manage a few of the simpler tray puzzles when he is sitting quietly on his own.

Television will begin to interest him, mainly because of the moving and eye-catching pictures, but you should be selective in what you let him see. As we have said before, lengthy periods of watching will certainly keep him quiet but are essentially passive and uncreative and will do nothing to help his development. However, there are some excellent short programmes specially devised for small children and these — and only these — are good for him. He will derive great satisfaction from recognizing the characters and the music and will become totally involved. You can, of course, enlarge on the stories afterwards and some of them appear in book form. These books are usually well and sensitively done and will afford him great pleasure.

But even the best television satisfies only two of his senses — sight and hearing — and there is all the difference in the world between a television apple and the real thing, with its texture, weight, smell and taste. Make sure television plays only a minor part in his day.

Sound

New sounds will be part of the total experience of new places he goes to and he will now associate sounds and the objects that make them quickly and easily. He will, in fact, be able to remember sounds properly and make an attempt to imitate them. 'Quack', 'Miaow', 'Wuff-wuff' and so on.

He will be able to turn handles with some skill and a musical box will fascinate him even if after a few minutes it has ceased to fascinate you. He will continue to enjoy his favourite gramophone records. Do not add to them too often. He will still prefer the old ones he knows well and can sing along with.

Touch

Up to now much of his play has been concerned with establishing the feel, shape and texture of things and dabbling with elemental substances like earth, sand and water. Now he will begin to play with more purpose. He will fill a bucket with sand so that he can carry it out of the sandpit to dump on the doorstep. He will dig holes, fill them with water, drop things into them and stir the muddy puddle with a stick, and you may hear him talking to himself as he stirs up this imaginary dinner.

He will find water a fascinating substance and he is well aware of its properties; he will love to pour himself 'tea' in a plastic cup from a toy teapot. In fact, he will find all water games interesting and he will want to help you wash up, wash the floor, water plants or participate in anything where water is poured or splashed about. He will also want to wash his own toys, dolls, dolls'-house and so on.

He will be aware of the texture of his clothes and may refuse to wear certain garments because he does not like the feel of them. On the other hand another piece of clothing may be loved more for its texture than its colour. He will love a teddy bear or similar soft toy and, indeed, a great many children become very attached to these toys, refusing to go to bed without them and using them as confidantes, talking to them, hugging them and generally treating them as living things. Another child will attach himself to an old bit of blanket or a nappy and derive great comfort from it, carrying it about with him wherever he goes. There seems to be a great need for a 'cuddly' at this stage.

Smell

He is now sure of which are nice and which nasty smells and will make his feelings clear with smiles or grimaces. He will also be able to guess what things are by their smells without being able to see them; he will be able to smell a packet or other object concealed in your hand and tell you what it is. This can sometimes be a good game when you have a boring wait in a shop, for instance. Don't forget that he will like you to join in the game too and test your skill in identifying smells correctly.

Taste

It is a good idea to try out as many new flavours and textures on him as you can. An interesting way of doing this is to play at tea parties with him and fill little plastic cups with new tastes — raw vegetables, little squares of bread with new spreads, dried fruit, cooked meat, etc.

Physical

At about this time, six months or so after he has learned to walk, your toddler will be able to aim his bottom at a chair and be sure that the chair remains in place when he turns his back on it. It is a fascinating spectacle to watch — the steady look to see that the chair is there, the turning of the back and the slow lowering of the body onto it. It shows splendid control and confidence.

He will be climbing the stairs upright, holding on to the banisters, but will still crawl down. He can run a little, even if rather flat-footedly. He will love to try his strength carrying things and will quietly climb onto anything he can reach. Also, like a kitten, he will not always know how to get down. In these circumstances it is better to show him how to get down himself rather than to lift him down: this way he will learn to manage on his own.

Social

This is a really sociable age. He will use his limited vocabulary on you all the time and follow you around the house imitating all the things that you do. He will want to be appreciated and praised for the help that he is giving you and will enjoy your pleasure at his improved skills. This is always a spur to effort. He will enjoy helping his parents too, washing the car, hanging up clothes, clearing the shed, gardening. Doing things with Daddy is important for all children: he takes them more for granted, treats them as more grown-up; plays with them more roughly and does not bother so much about the rules that are already beginning to dog his life with his mother. Perhaps the word 'rules' sounds over-stern with a child at this stage of his development but, of course, if a family is to live together in harmony there have to be a number of don'ts.

Although Daddy tends to be more relaxed about rules like this and Mummy has to bear the brunt of imposing them — simply because she is ever-present — they do give a child a necessary sense of order and permanence and after a session with his father, your child will be glad to get back to his mother and all the warmth and security she gives him.

He will like to have other children round him when he plays, but will not play with them yet. If they take away his toy he will try to grab it back or sit and howl. On the other hand if he hits another child and it cries he will watch it clinically, rather as though he had squeezed a squeaky toy, and may well repeat the blow to prolong this interesting spectacle. It must be remembered that the blow is not a sign of anger. This comes later when, for instance, he will hit another child to make him give back a toy. But at this present state of development he has no understanding of other people's feelings.

Practical suggestions

Sight

Sorting box
He will love to sort things out by their shape or texture: it is a good idea to get a large shallow box and put into it a variety of objects for him to sort — plastic cutlery, large buttons, cotton reels, bottle tops,

fir cones, conkers, keys, old playing cards and so on. Beware of putting in too many or the whole thing becomes a confusing jumble, but include several of each type of object. To prevent — hopefully — too much scatter of objects, a toy-tray is a useful addition.

Tray

Get a piece of hardboard 24″ x 18″ and stick a half-inch strip of wood round the edge. Cover the whole thing with a plain-coloured adhesive plastic. You will find this invaluable for many games and prevents too much overflow. It is also useful later on as a base on which to build models so that they do not have to be dismantled when they are moved.

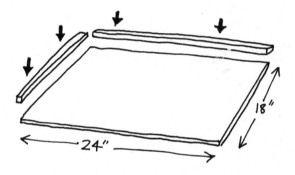

Cover with plain
coloured sticky-back
plastic

Discs on a stick

This attractive wooden or plastic toy consists of a circular base with a central stick on which is arranged a pyramid of coloured discs of decreasing size. At this age he will not be able to grade the discs properly but he will enjoy putting them on the stick and watching them slide down. This toy is inexpensive to buy or quite simple to make.

Simple jigsaw puzzles

You can buy jigsaw puzzles specially designed for tiny children, made of wood with inset pictures that can be lifted out and replaced. A little more difficult are the ones which consist of a wooden frame with an inner picture divided into four or five obvious pieces.

You can make your own simple puzzles by sticking a bold picture onto a piece of stiff card and cutting it into two or three large pieces. Incidentally, when you are making him a toy like this, always let him see you do it and 'help' if possible.

Jig saws

Posting-box

There are some very attractive posting-boxes on the market which are more challenging than the simple one described earlier. They consist of a box with differently shaped holes cut in the lid — circle, square, triangle, rectangle etc., and a number of wooden shapes that can only be posted through the proper hole. But you can make your own by cutting a square, a circle and a narrow slit in the top of a shoebox and giving him things — corks, wooden bricks, large buttons etc. — which will only go through their own holes.

Finger-painting

This is a wonderfully satisfying, messy game, highly creative and something he will enjoy doing until he is old enough to go to school. For it you need:

    A tray (either the one described earlier or a large tin
        tray or meat tin), or a formica-topped table.
    Protective clothing and covering for your child, the table,
        the floor, and, probably, you.
    A jelly made of cornflour and water or Polycel, coloured.
    To make this:
    1 Mix a tablespoonful of cornflour with a little
        cold water. Slowly add half a pint of boiling water
        and mix thoroughly.
    2 Into a jam jar of cold water put half a teaspoon of
        Polycel. Stir rapidly until the mixture sets.
    Add food colouring or poster paint (from art shops or stationers)
        and mix until the colour is evenly distributed.

Cover the table and the surrounding floor with newspaper and the child with an apron which covers his front and arms. Put a large dollop of jelly-paint on the tray and let him put his hands in it. He will spread it about, smack it, make patterns with it, use his palms and his fingers and generally have a whale of a time. He can be left to his own devices for some time but the moment his interest begins to flag clear it all away.

Water painting

Although he may not be ready yet for brushes and paint an excellent introduction is to let him paint with water outside on any suitable flat surface: doorstep, garden path, garage floor. He will get used to using a brush and, of course, the 'paintings' evaporate without trace.

This is a game that can be taken with you anywhere; all you need is a stout paintbrush and a plastic container of water. Walls, paths, even pavements are perfect canvases for water painting.

Sound

Musical shakers
You can discard his old rattles and let him help you to make some new ones. Any kind of plastic bottle, or two yoghurt pots taped together, mouth-to-mouth, can make a musical shaker. But this time let him choose what is to go inside and let him insert his chosen objects — dried peas, rice, sand, buttons, paper clips, lumps of sugar. He will enjoy hearing the different sounds they make (and finding out what he put inside them, given half a chance).

Shakers

Bells
Sew some little bells on a circular piece of elastic and slip it over his wrist from time to time. He will enjoy the noise it makes when he moves his arm.

Musical box

Now that he can turn a handle he will enjoy playing with a musical box. Choose a tune that will not drive you crazy because you will hear a lot of it!

Ring-a-ring of roses

He can now run about fairly proficiently and he will love holding your hands and playing 'Ring-a-ring of roses' with you, especially the falling down bit at the end. Lots of people can play this game and even grandfathers can fall down very effectively:

> Ring-a-ring of roses
> A pocket full of posies
> Atishoo! Atishoo!
> We all fall down.

Touch

Play dough

Small children adore playing with pastry and will go on doing so until well into their school years. So make him some of his own.

Take two cups of flour, half a cup of salt and a few drops of cooking oil. Mix to a pliable — but not sticky — dough with water. Add a few drops of food colouring to make it more interesting. With this play dough he can do all kinds of fascinating things. He will make his own pies, cakes and loaves very happily, and can safely be left on his own while he does it.

Kitchen tools

For playing with his play dough, let him have his own set of kitchen tools in his own little box. Give him a few plastic pastry cutters, a rolling pin (eight inches of a broom handle or one-inch dowelling is per-fect), a flour dredger made from a plastic jar with holes pierced in the lid, a patty tin and anything else suitable that you don't use very often. The play tray will stop the flour scattering too much. Play dough will last a week if kept in a plastic bag in a cool place.

Water play

Children at this stage will play with water whenever they are given the chance. During the summer this is easy: sit him outside with a bowl of water, wearing waterproof clothing or, better, nothing at all, and he will be perfectly happy.

Water toys

If the weather is bad or you don't have a suitable place for water play in the open air, cover part of the kitchen floor with newspaper, an old curtain, a blanket or anything absorbent and let him sit in the middle of it with a bowl of water. But in this case keep a careful eye on him. With his bowl of water he will want a collection of water toys. These are found in almost every home — plastic cups, washing-up liquid bottles (cut them in half; the bottom half makes a cup, the top half a funnel) and, in fact, any sort of plastic container. Bore a few holes in the base and sides so that the water runs out interestingly. Cups and teapots (unbreakable) and watering cans, real and miniature, are useful. He will have lots of instructive fun with a piece of rubber or plastic tubing that he can fit onto a plastic funnel. He will love wooden boats, corks and sponges.

Sorting-box

As well as a shape sorting-box, make him a texture sorting-box. In it place half a dozen or so two-inch cardboard discs or squares and cover them with a particular type of material. Make more sets covered with other textured or patterned fabrics — silk, cotton, velvet, towelling, hessian, sandpaper — use what you have available. He will find his own way of sorting them so let him make his own choice; don't show him.

Teddy bear

Most children already have a special cuddly toy by this age but if your child has not, now is the time to get him one.

Smell and taste

Tea-set

This is an excellent way of introducing new tastes and smells to him. Cut up new and interesting food into doll-sized pieces for him to serve on the little plates. Make sure that the tea-set is not too small and fiddly, and that the cups are big enough to get hold of. A plastic picnic set is a good idea.

Mustard and cress

There are several ways of growing cress seeds. One is to put a circle of blotting paper or other absorbent material in a saucer or plate, moisten it and sprinkle the seeds on it. Water it every day or it will dry out. Another is to put a little earth in a yoghurt pot and sow the seeds in this.

The seeds germinate very quickly and with a strong smell. He will

potato

cut the top off a potato
scoop out a hollow, sow the seeds.
Decorate the face.
This does not need watering
as the potato is moist enough.

eggshell

put a little earth in the
eggshell. Sprinkle on seeds.
Decorate with a felt pen.

almost certainly smell this of his own accord once he has been introduced to it. Best of all, after about a week the crop can be harvested
and eaten in a bread and butter sandwich (no crusts). A cress garden
like this should not be a perpetual thing, but it will always be remembered and greeted with great enthusiasm the next time the plate or
pot and seed packet are introduced.

Physical

Playground in the park

He is now old enough to go on the baby swings in the park or children's playground. When you push him stand in front of him so that
he can see you all the time. He will also enjoy riding on the rocking-
horse provided there are no big children on it to rock it too violently.
Park-keepers and attendants traditionally turn a blind eye on parents accompanying very small children on roundabouts and other
playground equipment.

Wheeled toys
Large wheeled toys to sit in and push with his feet are excellent at this stage. Other large wheeled toys that he can fill with bricks, earth, sand, etc., and push about are also very good for him. The baby walker he used when he was just tottering along can now be used for this.

Cardboard boxes
Never throw away a big cardboard box without letting him play with it first.

Big beads to thread
He may not be nimble enough to manage bead-threading yet, but there is no reason why he should not try. If he is really puzzled give him something else to play with and gently remove them when his attention is distracted. Bring them out again later. Beads can be bought but cotton reels are a good substitute. Make sure the string is thick and smooth and that the ends are not frayed. Bind them with Sellotape if necessary to give a firm threading end.

The tray will come in useful for keeping the beads in one place.

Social

Telephone
A toy telephone is very useful at this stage when he is starting to imitate the things you do.

Dolls' bed and covers
A few little blankets or shawls are useful to wrap round his dolls or teddy so that he can tuck them into bed (a shoe box does well) and scold, cuddle or otherwise talk to them. Any old pieces of material will do, cut to about a foot square.

Watering can
This is very useful if you have somewhere outside where he can play. You can see him copying you and pretending it is anything from a tea-pot to a petrol pump. You will find that he can make imaginative use of all kinds of mundane household articles and they all operate as things which expand his social abilities.

Fingerplays

Here's the church and here's the steeple
Open the doors and see the people
Here's the parson going upstairs
Here's the parson saying his prayers.

This finger play uses the fingers to illustrate steeple, people, parson and pulpit, and is easy to do. It is, however, rather difficult to explain in words and if you were never taught it, or have forgotten how to do it, we suggest you ask a child for a demonstration.

This is the house with its chimney-pot tall
This is the tree that hangs over the wall
This is the window, open it wide
Here are the children, peeping outside.

The first line of this has the finger movement as the previous rhyme. The second line is accompanied by making a 'wall' of one hand by holding it horizontally and a 'tree' of the other by putting it vertically over the wall. For the third line make a hole by putting the tip of your thumb and forefinger together and for the fourth line pop the fore and middle fingers of the other hand through the 'window' and wiggle them about.

Up the cold white candlestick
Crept little Mousey Brown
To steal and eat the candlewax
But he could not get down
So he called for his Grandma
'Grandma, Grandma!'
But Grandmas was in town
So he curled himself into a ball
And rolled himself right down.

One hand upright to make candlestick. The fingers of the other hand 'run up' the candlestick and sit on the top. They stay there until the 'curling into a ball' line when the hands are rotated round each other downwards.

A tiny, tiny worm
Wriggled along like this
Without a sound

90

It came to a tiny hole
A tiny hole in the ground
It wriggled right inside
Without a sound.

Here the worm is the index finger of one hand which wriggles into the hole made by loosely clenching the other.

Here's a ball for baby
Big and soft and round

(The hands overlap to make a ball)

Here is baby's hammer
See how he can pound

(The clenched fist makes hammering movements).

Here is baby's music
Clapping, clapping so

(The hands are clapped)

Here are baby's soldiers
Standing in a row

(The hands are held upright, palm outwards)

Here is her umbrella
To keep our baby dry

(An imaginary umbrella is held up)

Here is baby's cradle
To rock a baby-bye.

(The arms are folded and rocked)

And for this last one the appropriate parts of the body are touched and the hands clapped:

Heads and shoulders, knees and toes
Knees and toes, knees and toes
Hands and shoulders, knees and toes
We all clap hands together.

91

7 'I Am Me'

By this stage your child is able to do a great deal for himself and he has a grasp of language that enables him to communicate quite well. He is intensely curious and anxious to try out anything and everything that he sees other people doing. But there is now one big development: he is beginning to recognize his limitations and this makes him terribly frustrated, often producing uncontrollable tantrums.

All children go through this stage to a greater or lesser extent. With some it is hardly perceptible, being no more than a slightly heightened crossness when it comes to putting on shoes, going to bed or not being allowed a sweet. But with others both mother and child end the day exhausted after a series of battles over everything — wanting fish fingers, not wanting fish fingers, going upstairs, shutting the door, picking up a toy. This can go on for months and it is small consolation to the mother to know that it is quite normal and that her screaming, struggling infant will eventually grow up into a normal and even-tempered human being.

This stage is, in fact, a vital — if traumatic — advance towards maturity and marks the child's discovery of himself as an individual. It is the time that he realizes he has a will and that he can alter the course of events. He can make other human beings react — especially Mummy — and he has an irresistible urge to use this new-found power. It is now for the first time that he becomes extremely possessive about his own things and his own people. They are 'mine'. He will have been conscious of this word for some time, but, quite suddenly, it is pregnant with meaning.

This is also the time when he sees his father as a threat to his relationship with his mother and this can be very puzzling and worrying because, of course, Daddy is also a passionately loved figure. But the signs are clear and rather touching. You will find, for instance, your child wriggling in between you when he has a morning cuddle.

But his instinctive jealousy is not confined to his father: it will be shown to anyone or anything that takes his mother's attention away — the new baby, the telephone, the sewing machine — and it is no accident that when Mummy goes to the lavatory there is very often an insistent clamour on the other side of the door, demanding her attention there and then.

A favourite place for a tantrum is the sweetshop or supermarket when the busy mother says, 'No, we don't want one of those,' when expensive cans are piled into the trolley or 'No, you can't have a biscuit till we get home.' This can be very embarrassing, especially to young mothers with first babies. They notice the stares of other shoppers and feel that these reflect on their success as mothers. Older and more experienced onlookers will smile and remember.

When this happens there are two courses open to you: you can give in quickly to avoid fuss and embarrassment, or you can let him scream his head off while you calmly (or apparently calmly) find something to distract him. If you take the easy way out and choose the first course of action you are building up trouble for yourself because he will quickly realize that you will give in to his demands if he makes a fuss. The firm approach is best because in spite of his fury it gives him the assurance that life is governed by comfortingly stable rules and also confidence in the confining word 'No'. After a while nearly all children are prepared to bargain, to wait until later — so long as you consistently keep to your half of the bargain.

But, to be fair, it is hard to keep cool when your child is in the middle of a public tantrum. Each of our own four children has been removed screaming when refused an instant sweet. But it has only had to be done once or twice. As soon as they realized that the occasional sweet they were allowed was only given them at home and never in a shop that particular tantrum ceased.

An extra difficulty arises because at this stage a child has not sufficient command of language to explain to you exactly what it is he wants. This often results in your giving the wrong answer or doing the wrong thing, which inevitably makes a tense situation even worse.

But the situation must not be exaggerated: he will not be screaming all the time. By now, in fact, he has surprising powers of concentration. We found our children particularly good at applying lipstick, cutting dolls' or their own hair and turning bathroom taps on — though never off. One of the most familiar results of a child's powers of concentration at this stage is the meticulous and large-scale removal of wallpaper. Any tiny tear gives them the opportunity of getting their fingernails into it and from then on they can be absorbed for hours in a stripping job that would shame a professional decorator. It really is silly to slap a small child in these circumstances. Quite apart from the fact that he might well be virtuously imitating Daddy, nobody has ever told him that pulling off wallpaper is wrong and — as you can imagine — it is a very fascinating activity. If you are really concerned about the innocent destructiveness of your child, always make sure that you have him in sight when he is playing.

It is very important that a child builds up a picture of what may and may not be done in a very confusing world. What is right one day is wrong the next; what one person is praised for another is blamed for. It is good to imitate Daddy in some things but not in others. Be sure that if you make rules you stick to them. This gives him confidence and reassures him there are fixed points in this shifting universe.

Remember to find plenty of time for cuddles. He has to come to terms with a bewildering world and your love and understanding are essential to him. Always spend part of your day sitting or playing with him and on no account miss the bedtime story.

At about this time you may decide that he is nearly ready for a playgroup or nursery school. He is beginning to cope with his surroundings without fighting them all the time, and this means that he will be prepared to leave you for short spells because he understands and accepts that you will always be there when he comes back. In fact you may well find that home is getting a little restrictive for him on occasions and that he needs extra stimulus for his curiosity and imagination.

Things your child needs at this stage

Creative play

He will be playing creatively with everything that comes his way and he should be given every opportunity to sit and cut things (with round-ended children's scissors), stick things, paint things, draw on things. He will probably produce nothing recognizable in any of these activities but he will be kept happily and most constructively occupied for hours.

He should be allowed to go on with all the messy play he is still enjoying. Earth is a particularly satisfying substance to play with, especially when you add water. It can be splashed on walls like cement or you can make mud pies. Sand too is good to play with, and it is possible for him to have some kind of sand-play in even the smallest and tidiest flat.

It is wise to avoid things that are too difficult. If he has trouble with jigsaws, threading beads, sticking boxes together or other tasks which seem simple enough to adults, give him something easier to do. But most of the things that frustrate him are connected with his workaday world, not his toys.

Imaginative play

At this stage he will project his own experiences onto his dolls and other toys. This sort of play develops fully over the next couple of years and many children live imaginary lives quite distinct from the real world. From the earliest days of recognizing his own individuality you will see him 'being' someone else, imitating them and acting in the way they do. He doesn't need a great deal to stimulate his imagination now — perhaps a cardboard policeman's helmet or a flowered hat and a long skirt to dress up in, a few small saucepans to do 'real' cooking in with beads and stones over an imaginary cooker.

His dolls and soft toys will still be played with and talked to as if they were alive and you will almost certainly hear him repeating things to them that he has heard himself, 'Naughty teddy', 'Don't do that', 'Eat that up, dear'. Discerning parents can learn quite a lot about themselves and how they speak if they listen carefully to these private conversations.

He may begin to have irrational fears and nightmares and it is best to take his imaginary monsters seriously. Leave his door open at night with the light on outside or, if necessary, leave him with a low wattage bedside light with a red or blue bulb, to give him the extra comfort and security he needs.

He will love looking at books and following a simple story in them. The ones he will like best will be about the everyday things that happen to him and that he sees about him — shopping trips, food, toys, his family. He can immediately relate to these things. So he will enjoy books illustrated with things he can recognize and name, and special books with illustrations of favourite rhymes and songs.

Physical

He is now growing steadily more confident in his own physical capabilities. He will love to run, crawl, roll and climb and he will need big and bulky things to push and pull about. He will tackle the climbing frame and the slide, will love to climb a small ladder and be the foreman or the window cleaner. He will sit on a pedal bike and begin to work out how to ride it. He will be able to kick a ball and throw it but he will not yet be able to catch it. He will also be a great deal more dexterous with his fingers and perform many complicated manipulations with great speed and accuracy. It is sensible not to give his small fingers tasks which are beyond them: violent frustration often follows.

Social

He is not ready yet to play co-operatively with children of his own age, although as he gets older he will be quite happy to play side by side with a contemporary and not feel compelled to take the other child's toys away from him. The same track will do for both their trains or the same table for both their pieces of pastry and rolling pins. But he may enjoy being played with by older children and, as the baby, being pushed about in a pram, dressed up and put to bed like a doll.

He still needs Mummy, and plenty of love and approval, although he may be prepared to leave her quite happily for short periods.

Practical suggestions

Sight

Books

We have already suggested the kind of books a child at this stage likes to look at, but, however much loved some old favourites are, parents will introduce new ones when they think the time is ripe. What you choose is a matter of instinct or trial and error; your child will teach you. Luckily there is a range of books of several different kinds — pictures only, pictures with captions, pictures connected in a story, a story with incidental illustrations.

Picture books   There are a number of beautifully produced and illustrated ABC books on the market, many by well-known artists. We always found one of these worth investing in but, of course, they can be borrowed from most children's libraries. Smaller and cheaper books with good, simple illustrations are also available in most bookshops. Cheap books sold in the local stationer or department store should generally be avoided or, at least, looked at carefully, as they often have poor pictures.

Story books   Choose simple stories without too many words on a page and heavily illustrated so that your child can easily follow the story while he sits on your knee. Children love the re-telling of an everyday event. The hardback versions of good storybooks are quite expensive but many have been reprinted in paperback which are excellent for your child's bookshelf.

Storybooks without words   There are a number of books on the market which tell a story without words. They consist of a series of pictures with an obvious sequence that Mummy, Daddy or even the child himself can describe. It is good fun giving the various characters names that he knows.

Nursery rhymes   There are several collections of nursery rhymes, some with first-class illustrations. It is a good idea here to escape from the bold coloured pictures which are his staple fare and choose something completely different, e.g., pen and ink drawings with fine details, complicated pre-Raphaelite-type illustrations, etc. They will recognize the rhyme from the 'black sheep' in the illustration and go on to look for other fascinating things in the pictures. Books like this are often treasured right through childhood.

Library books Children can usually join the junior library when they are five. Nearly all libraries allow you to take out children's books on your own ticket. We also found that librarians at junior libraries are remarkably tolerant about accidental tears, fingermarks and jam stains.

At about this age your child will love a visit to the junior library where he can sit and look at some of the beautiful books with you and even say which ones he wants you to borrow.

Paint

You may have been tempted to introduce painting already or you may not be prepared to start it yet. In any case it is at about this stage of your child's development that he will be ready to enter the fabulous world of applying colour to paper.

You need:

Powder paint From the art shop or good toy shop or bought through the post from any of the big artists' materials manufacturers. Poster paint is equally good but more expensive. Restrict your choice to the three primary colours — red, blue and yellow. When he is older you can add black and white and, if you wish, other colours, but this is not really necessary.

Brushes Hog-hair brushes are best, one for each colour, size 18. There can also be obtained from the art shop or artists' materials manufacturer. They are long-handled with thick, strong bristles.

Paint pots You can use jam jars but remember these break easily. Stand them in a wire milk bottle crate or shoe-box that will hold them without tipping. Yoghurt cups are too shallow and the long brushes make them tip up. A good idea is to cut a washing-up liquid bottle in half and insert the top half upside down into the bottom half to make an unspillable container like the old fashioned glass inkwells. Or you can buy plastic non-tip paintpots.

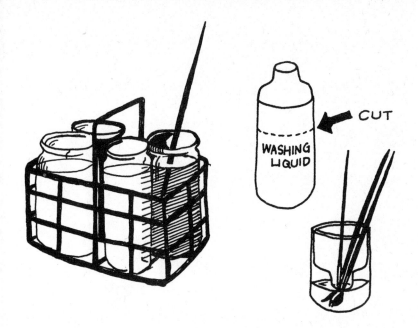

Paper   Any paper will do. Plain wrapping paper, wallpaper (get a sample book from your local decorator if you can), opened-up paper bags. We often used newspaper: big sheets, free and splendidly absorbent.

Apron   Make this yourself from some waterproof material. It must be a coverall: small children are geniuses at finding any chinks you have left in their armour. Another useful trick is to turn a little shirt back to front. If your child has no elder brother or cousins a suitable shirt can be picked up for a few pence at a jumble sale.

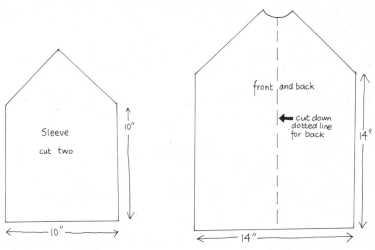

Sleeve

cut two

10"

10"

front and back

← cut down dotted line for back

14"

14"

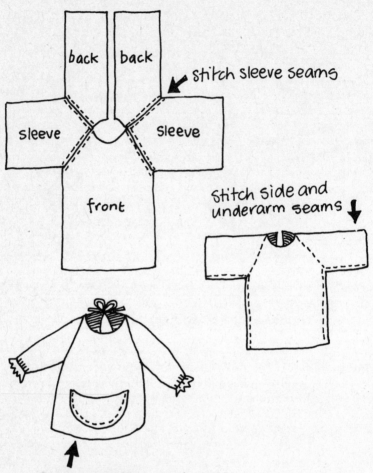

back back

stitch sleeve seams

sleeve sleeve

front

Stitch side and
underarm seams

Turn up cuffs and insert
a piece of elastic to fit
child's wrist. Turn in
back seam and turn up
hem. Bind neck with
bias binding, leave two
long ends to tie. Add a
big pocket if you wish.

Preparation Mix a tablespoonful of the powder paint to a thick paste with a very little water. The colour should be thick and dramatic. Later, if he uses a lot of paint, you can economize by thickening it with Polycel or even flour.

Either let your child paint directly onto paper on the floor (which you have previously covered with plenty of newspaper) or let him kneel up and paint on the table, also suitably covered. The universal tray comes in handy here too. Prop it up and make him an easel; the rim will prevent the paper sliding down. Or you can persuade someone to buy him an easel for a Christmas or birthday present. This makes a wonderful gift — if you have storage space, and preferably other children to pass it on to. Or, again, an easel is quite straightforward to make. Clip the paper on with clothes pegs.

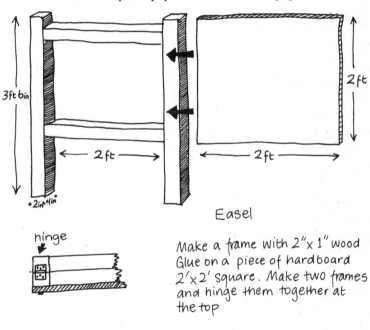

Easel

Make a frame with 2"x 1" wood Glue on a piece of hardboard 2'x2' square. Make two frames and hinge them together at the top

101

Clearing away   As soon as he begins to lose interest, put the paint pots away. If the paint in them is still clean, cover it and it can be used again. Wash the brushes in cold water and stand them bristle end up to dry. Be sure to hang at least one of his paintings up where he can see it and the family can admire it.

Crayons
Make sure he has big fat crayons. Keep them in a special box or tin where he can find them and put them away.

Picture Lotto
This is a matching game he will love to play with you or by himself. All you have to do is to find lots of duplicate pictures (identical advertisements are particularly useful) and cut them out — two dogs, two aeroplanes, two babies and so on. They should be about 3″ x 4″ in size.

Take two pieces of card about 8″ x 6″ and stick one set of pictures on each. Then cut one card into quarters. The game is for him to match the pieces to the card by covering them correctly.

You can make lots of these sets. You can also buy picture lotto sets, but make sure that the pictures are large enough. The bought sets with nine pictures per card are really more suitable for older children.

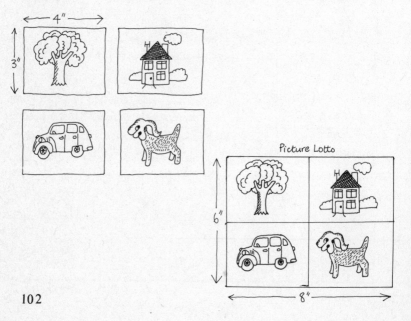

Picture Lotto

Sound

Poetry and nursery rhyme anthology

Small children love the sound and music of words and as they get older you will often hear them rhyming words for themselves. If you have a book of rhymes with attractive illustrations you can go through them together repeating the rhymes and rhythm so that he builds up a large repertoire of these satisfying sounds, for example:

> 'Bubble' said the kettle. 'Bubble' said the pot.
> 'Bubble bubble bubble, we are very very hot.'
> 'Shall I take you off the fire?'
> 'No, you needn't trouble
> This is just the way we talk, bubble, bubble, bubble.'

Trumpet or whistle

Now is the time to get him something to blow that will make a good solid sound. There are plenty of pipes and whistles made of wood that make a satisfying but not too penetrating noise.

Touch

Sand

If you have a garden, now is the time to think of a sandpit. It doesn't need to be elaborate: an old drawer or a zinc or plastic bath sunk in the ground is perfectly suitable, although many parents find it easy enough to make something a little larger and more professional-looking. Get a load of silver sand from the local builder, making sure you don't buy too much (a mistake all too easily made as we found to our cost: our small garden looked like Bondi beach for months afterwards). If you explain exactly what you want it for he will advise you.

Keep your child's sandpit covered with a chicken-wire frame or other semi-permanent construction, otherwise it will quickly become the local cats' and dogs' public lavatory, and threadworm is very easily caught this way. If you have the sandpit indoors cover the floor with an old curtain or blanket. A candlewick bedspread is good as the sand gets caught in the channels.

Stock your sandpit with plastic and rubber buckets and spades but don't forget that as far as your child is concerned plastic cups and wooden spoons are just as much fun. Keep the sand damp so that he can shape it and mould it.

Dry sand

If you are brave enough a box of dry sand is fascinating. It is preferably played with outside because it is undoubtedly messy. But dry sand has quite different properties from damp sand; it is much more like water and great fun to pour. To do this properly you need a sieve, funnel, strainer, spoons, plastic cups, tiny bottles and other containers. The tray is useful.

Oatmeal

A heap of oatmeal will make less mess than sand if played with indoors and is almost as satisfactory. It can be swept up, packed away in a tin and used again and again. Have patty tins, small containers and spoons for this. Other alternatives to dry sand are salt, rice, lentils, etc. None of these spreads all over the place as badly as sand. Again, the tray is useful to prevent the worst of the scattering.

Sticking things

The best paste for young children to stick things with is undoubtedly Polycel. Mix a jarful and put some into a yoghurt cup or something similar with a cheap paste brush. At first he will just enjoy painting paper, boxes and other suitable objects with this gooey stuff, but as he watches you pasting pictures down he will try to copy you.

It will require quite a lot of thought for him to work out and understand that it is the *back* of the pictures that needs pasting and not the front; but once this lesson is learned it is never forgotten.

Pictures cut out from magazines, Christmas cards, colourful circulars — any kind of picture is suitable and will keep him happily sticking. Don't mind if they are all stuck one on top of the other with unbelievable quantities of paste. Whatever the result, treat it with genuine interest.

Cutting

He may have mastered the art of using scissors (round-ended children's scissors, that is) to cut things like dolls' hair, or even his own, but he still may be quite unable to squeeze the blades together to cut shapes out of paper or thin card. But imitation and practice make perfect and if he is given sufficient material he will soon learn. Illustrations and advertisements from the colour supplements and other similar magazines are ideal. When he is not actually using the scissors under your supervision keep them well out of his reach. If he enjoys cutting up magazines he will equally enjoy cutting up the mail, your books or the notes in your wallet.

Smell and taste

Helping in the kitchen
The desire to copy you in everything you do is now in full spate and you may as well make the most of it. It is more sensible — and less wearing on your nerves — to put him in a safe corner with something simple and useful to do than to keep telling him to get out from under your feet.

He will be full of 'what' questions — 'What's that?' 'What's in there?' so you will be increasing his vocabulary while he tastes and smells and makes things. Remember that boys enjoy this sort of helping every bit as much as girls, so don't try to differentiate between the sexes. This kind of distinction arrives, alas, all too soon. While he is helping, let him taste and smell anything he wants to. In any case, it will be almost impossible to stop him.

Helping in the garden
The garden, not surprisingly, is another place full of interesting smells and tastes. He will love to do simple jobs and even really tough ones like carrying big stones and branches. Show him seeds and plants but insist very firmly that he asks you before he eats any of them. Don't forget that many of the most colourful and succulent-looking seeds and berries are highly poisonous.

Helping with the car
This is another activity full of interesting sounds and differing smells: petrol, oil, upholstery, leather, rubber. Keep his fingers away from anything dangerous by giving him a job like polishing to do while Daddy does the actual tinkering. Again the 'What's that?' questions will flow. Be sure you answer him.

Physical

Pedal bike

About now, somewhere around his third birthday, he will be ready for his first pedal bike and it is worth spending a little time, trouble and money to get one which really suits him and is strong, firm and safe. At first he will not be able to turn the pedals with his feet and will push it along with his feet on the ground. But he will soon learn to pedal it properly and from then on it will be a favourite occupation. Take it with you to the park — it can quite easily be hitched to the pushchair or pram. Never take him shopping on his pedal bike. If you want to know why, take him once and find out. It is an experiment you will not want to repeat.

Keep the bike clean and oiled, or, rather, let him help do this — it's a job he will enjoy. On his fourth birthday buy him a bell for the bike ... once he has mastered the technique of pedalling he'll enjoy the added interest which a bell will provide.

Ball

This is the stage where he will really begin to appreciate a ball, although he has probably been playing with one for some time. Get him a ball about eight inches in diameter that is colourful, bouncy and not too heavy. He will love throwing it and running after it and will adore a romping ball game with a grown-up. You will find him very possessive about his own ball: he will not be at all willing to relinquish it to another child because he will want to hold it all the time. When other children are there it is really much more sensible to let each have a ball of his own.

Simple construction toys

Look out for construction toys that are strong, simple and adaptable and which can be added to. They will then go on being used when your child is much older. Construction toys like Lego — hard plastic shapes which fit firmly together — will start exercising his imagination as well as his fingers and it will remain a favourite throughout his childhood.

Cubes, spheres and wheels with holes in them into which rods can be banged are a good buy at this stage.

Bricks
Check through his supply of bricks. You may wish to add to them to give more variety — long strips of wood for bridges, slopes and paths, cylinders to roll about. Keep his bricks in a separate container, ideally a wooden box on wheels which can double as a cart.

Train set
This is another toy beloved of both boys and girls — lines to join together and a train or cars to push along and over. There are plastic train sets on the market; check that the rails are firm and will not buckle under tough usage. Extra pieces of equipment like bridges and turntables can be added to the basic set later on.

If you have a rich relation, you might suggest the wooden peg set, which fits together very firmly, for a present. It can be used for many layouts. It will, incidentally, last for your grandchildren.

Slide
He will now be pretty confident at climbing up things and will probably like to imitate the older children on the slide. He will still be too young to use the big slide in the park but will enjoy the miniature one about four or five feet high.

Social

Dressing up
Give him — if you can — a few clothes to make him look like the milkman, Grandma, Mummy, Daddy, etc. A long skirt, an old hat, a frilly petticoat, an overall, will be enough at this stage. Later on you can add bridal veil, handbag, spectacle frames, scarf, etc.

Wendy house
Games involving the imitation of people around him will continue for several years and you will find that he likes to get into a special corner that is his own private 'house'. Even in the smallest flat it is possible to pull out an armchair so that there is a secret corner for his family of dolls and a few books. Or you can throw a rug over the dining-room table so that it hangs down to make a cosy den. You can also make a screen from a clothes airer covered with material.

This versatile 'house' can be erected in any corner, indoors or out, and folds quite flat.

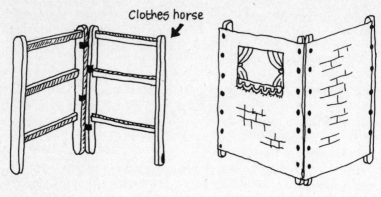

Clothes horse

Counting

Your child will already have started counting. There are a great number of counting rhymes that he can use to help himself, whether he is counting the stairs or the pictures in a book or whatever. Here are some examples:

> Six fat sausages frying in the pan
> All of a sudden one went Bang!
> Five fat sausages . . . etc.

Do a loud clap for 'Bang!' You can fry imaginary sausages or even play this as an eating-up-your-dinner game with the bits of food left on the plate. On this interesting Jack Sprat topic we always used the following to ensure a clean plate:

> Ha ha ha, here we go
> Five little ducklings in a row
> Ha ha ha, here we go
> Five little ducks go to and fro
> To and fro.

Then four, three, two and so on. To this day our children call small pieces of apple 'Ha ha ha!' A tip — remember that children are unable to subtract at this stage, so at the end of each verse always count *forward* the remaining fingers or objects, 'One two three four' etc., to establish that there really are the number needed to start the next verse.

Which hand?

All children love guessing games. Hide something in one clenched hand and let them guess which one. There is an old rhyme which goes with this:

> Handy, dandy, riddle me so
> Which hand will you have, high or low?

They also adore forcing your hand open to see if they guessed correctly.

Part 2

8 The Later Stages

The intention of this book so far has been to highlight the progressive stages of an infant's development and to describe ways in which it can be speeded and strengthened. It has told how his senses, his physical skills and his speech are refined stage by stage and how his individuality as a small human being is established. As explained in the introduction, easily identifiable physical stages of development have been preferred to chronological age.

At about the age of three your child will have mastered all his basic skills. He can walk, climb, manipulate and, in fact, has control of his body. He can dress himself, go to the lavatory, and is independent of adults in nearly all his normal activities. He has come to terms with his environment and does not dissolve into paroxysms of rage when it refuses to do what he wants it to. Most important of all, he can communicate. He has a vocabulary of several hundred words and can express his ideas and needs clearly and logically as well as listening carefully to yours and those of other people. He is confident enough in his own personality to be able to leave his mother and even the whole family for short periods. He knows now that his mother exists independently of him and experience has taught him that she will always be there when he returns. He is, in fact, a highly complex and efficient little animal.

The next two years before he starts his infant schooling will be spent in improving and perfecting, exploring and consolidating. There will be no more dramatic changes until he is ready to start school and make the first steps towards a life separate from his mother.

Because no marked physical developments occur in these next two years it seemed more sensible to arrange these final four chapters under more situational headings. Chapter Nine, 'Making things', gives you some ideas about the kinds of things he can do with his hands and how you can keep him happily and creatively occupied. Naturally both his manipulative and co-ordinating skills will be strengthened and improved at the same time. Chapter Ten, 'Playing with other children', gives you ideas for when he is with other children and about how his social skills are reinforced. Chapter Eleven, 'Those endless questions', is concerned with his intellectual development (in so far as this can be isolated from any other of his achievements) and gives you some clue as to how you can satisfy his voracious appetite for information by teaching him to find out for himself. Finally Chapter Twelve, 'Off to school', rounds up the book by helping you to prepare him for this next great step by ensuring that he is a confident and self-reliant child, socially at ease and able to conceptualize. Most important, once again, that a child should have been talked to throughout its entire first five years and thus be able to communicate effectively.

But before embarking on these chapters a few points need to be made. They concern things that could well affect your child's life and it is as well to discuss them at the beginning.

Nursery School or playgroup

Although the pressure for more playgroups and nursery schools is growing it will still be years before all our children have the benefit of this kind of pre-school education. This is a pity because playgroups and nursery schools offer an ideal environment for the three to five-year-olds and have everything necessary to help children to develop their physical skills, to enlarge their imaginations and to improve their social sensibilities. This offers them enormous advantages when they start 'big school'. They settle down to work immediately and quite naturally, while the child who has never simultaneously been away from its mother and with large numbers of other children can often find the experience traumatic and have difficulty in adjusting to it.

It therefore makes good sense for the parents of small children to press their local education authority and, indeed, the government of the day to provide more nursery classes. But, recognizing that your child may well have children of his own before they become universal, there is still much that parents can do.

The playgroup movement is a case in point. This was founded

because a number of mothers got together and decided that if the State would not provide pre-school education for their children they would do it themselves. Over the years the movement has expanded and it can now offer valuable advice to parents who are anxious that their children should have the advantages of pre-school education but are not sure how to go about getting it for them. If you would like to know how to form and run a playgroup, write to the Pre-School Playgroup Association, Alford House, Aveline Street, London SE 11 (01 582 8871): they will be glad to help you.

The playgroup is usually run in a church hall which has to be adapted for the children's use and the equipment stored away after each session. Parents pay their share of the cost of the hall, the equipment and the trained supervisor.

The type of equipment and the fundamental thinking behind nursery schools and playgroups is the same. The difference is the permanence of the layout and the appropriateness of the setting. Both give the children a freedom and scope they could not have at home. Climbing frame and slide, bikes and pushcarts, sand and water, clay and paint, construction toys and puzzles, cooking, a home corner, dressing-up box and books — all these are there for the children to use. They make models from junk — pictures from cereal packets, dolls from toilet roll tubes. They dance, sing and listen to stories. They have room to run around and shout in safety — indoors and out. Apart from these similarities State nursery classes have another edge over playgroups: they are run by a trained nursery teacher and a trained nursery assistant — and they are free.

But assuming that a nursery class is not available and a playgroup is, what should a conscientious parent look for? First, don't worry about the surroundings. Playgroups have to make the best of what they can get and the dingiest church hall can house the happiest and most efficient playgroup. Check that the children are allowed to play freely with sand, water, clay and paint. Secondly, make sure they are *not* taught to read and write. Provided they have plenty of creative and imaginative things to do and that there are plenty of good books to look at they will learn more about words and language than if they were forced to sit down and be formally taught their ABC. In the majority of cases five years is quite early enough to begin to learn to read and write, and children will then do so easily. But if the child himself shows an interest in reading, let him tackle the books he loves and knows by heart. If he wants new books, choose ones with plenty of rhyme and repetition. One excellent series, by Dr Seuss, uses basic words and plays with them in a very amusing way.

Outings

The more opportunities you can give your child to go to new places, and to experience new sights, sounds, smells and atmospheres, the better.

He will get much more fun from a trip if you discuss it with him first. For instance, if you are going to a zoo or wild-life sanctuary get a book about the animals that are there, talk about them, describe them and make sure he knows their names. If you are taking him to meet someone at the railway station, tell him what to expect and he will make much more of the experience: moreover, he will not be frightened by the noise and bustle. A boring trip to the hairdresser — where you sit for ages under the dryer — can become really interesting if he knows beforehand that there will be things to look at, to listen for and to smell. Never forget that things which are familiar and unnoticed by you can offer a wealth of new experience to him. Garage, yard, greenhouse, café, library, chemist, church — all are treasure-houses to a greedy young mind.

Journeys

A long journey with under-fives can be a nightmare — especially if mother is travelling alone with the children. Experience has taught us that careful preparation can do much to take the edge off — although it would be foolish to pretend that six hours on a slow train with an active four-year-old can ever be a bed of roses!

Pack a bag with magazines and scissors, felt pen, stiff (not liquid) paste and a scrapbook. This will keep an older child happy for a useful length of time. For younger children, nesting plastic cups and some big beads and a threader can be used in numerous ways. Imagination will suggest additions and variations.

'I-Spy' games — 'I spy something red', 'I spy something wooden', 'I spy something silver' — can break up the monotony of a journey and get children looking out of the window for fences, shop-fronts, churches, cars and so on.

Take plastic bags for gathering up the debris and in case of sudden sickness. Take a damp flannel in a plastic bag for wiping sticky faces and fingers. Never dress a child in decent clothes for a long journey: there is no known way of keeping an active child off the floor for at least part of the way.

Illness

Nowadays doctors are not so insistent that children stay in bed when they are ill, provided that they are kept in a warm room, in warm clothes and out of draughts. A really sick child will not want to get up in any case. The problems really arise with a convalescent child who demands your constant attention.

Many of the suggestions in Chapter Nine, 'Making things', will be useful in keeping him occupied, and he will enjoy making jigsaws he knows well and looking at his favourite books. Remember that a sick or convalescent child tires easily so intersperse these activities with frequent rests. Remove the game or book, brush the pieces of paper and crumbs from his sheets, plump up his pillow and settle him down with a favourite soft toy or teddy. When he shows signs of livening up again you can produce another interesting book or game.

It is a good idea to bring your chores to his room whenever possible and to rearrange your day so that, for instance, you sew during the day rather than in the evening. Ironing, preparing vegetables, mending and writing letters can all be done when you are with him and some of these domesticities can be combined with telling him a story or listening to a gramophone record.

Fears and nightmares

At this stage it is hard to distinguish between reality and fantasy. A chance remark, a picture in a magazine, something on the television, can easily make him worried or frightened because he has misinterpreted it and, for instance, thinks that what he has seen is going to happen to him and his family. So if he suddenly appears afraid of the dark or of going into a room by himself, don't chide him or laugh at him — go with him and try to find out what is worrying him. A dim light in his room or even a torch he can get hold of will often help.

Nightmares can be terribly real and frightening even to adults who *know* it was all only a dream. A drink, a trip to the lavatory, a cuddle and gentle understanding should settle him down again.

You will often find small children playing out their fears and experiences. When our youngest son was three he saw a frightening 'Thunderbirds' television programme where alligators grew to an enormous size and waddled round knocking down houses with their tails. This impressed him immensely and next day Mummy, who was running a playgroup at the time, found him and several other children busy making clay alligators. They did this obsessively for several days and Patrick finally produced such a splendidly ferocious model that it was glazed and fired: it remains a houshold ornament to this day. Several years later, Mummy's nursery class suddenly produced a similar spate of clay alligators. There had, of course, been a repeat of the programme.

Going to hospital

A visit to a hospital, clinic or dentist can be a frightening experience, sometimes necessarily accompanied by pain. Make sure he is familiar with what is going to happen so that it isn't too strange for him — show him books with doctors and nurses, stethoscopes and other instruments. Tell him what the doctor will do and tell him that you will stay with him all the time. Find out first that you *can* do this. You almost always can, but you may just possibly run into a reactionary backwater. If so you have a clear choice: either take him somewhere else or create such hell that they finally back down and allow you to stay.

After a visit to hospital or somewhere similar, talk about it when you get home. Let him play games about it, give him a white shirt as a doctor's coat and make him a stethoscope from string and buttons. Give him medicine for his dolls and something to 'inject' them with. Next time the visit will not be so traumatic.

Tidiness

When you consider the state of many playrooms and living-rooms you might think that children are naturally untidy. But parents seldom stop to consider where the blame often lies — squarely on their own shoulders. Nearly all the time children just have nowhere to *put* anything.

Putting up a few big, firm shelves is easy and putting toys and other objects away on them can become part of a game.

Storage boxes are easily come by and gallon-sized ice cream tubs are excellent for sorting out various types of toy bricks, puzzles, construction toys and so on. They look best if they are of a regular size; you do not need the lids. Transparent plastic food containers and shoeboxes labelled and painted come in useful. Keep the boxes mended. Broken boxes are useless and should be promptly thrown away. There are plenty more where those came from.

He can help decorate his storage boxes with pictures. And if he is fortunate enough to have a child's chest of drawers, he can put a picture of what's inside on each of the dozen or so drawers — crayons, farm animals, beads, Lego, etc.

Give him a special shelf for his own books if you can. Encourage him to close his books when he has finished with them and to put them away carefully. Books are going to be important to him throughout his life and he should learn early how to look after them properly.

Put loops on his dressing-up clothes so that they can be hung up and provide hooks at a convenient height for them. If he goes to nursery school or playgroup he will be used to putting things away — cash in on it.

9 Making Things

If your child is fortunate enough to go to a playgroup or nursery school it is likely that he will have come across many of the activities and materials mentioned in this chapter — and, indeed, in earlier ones. Playgroup and nursery school techniques are designed for children at this stage of their development and nothing but good can come of learning from them or stealing their ideas. Don't be afraid that your child will become bored by using the same material over and over again. If you look closely you will see him grow in proficiency and ingenuity. You will see that the same materials and activities are enjoyed by much older children who will, of course, be producing much more sophisticated models. Your child will learn to use the various materials to make exactly what he wants exactly the way he sees it — a big advance on just playing with the material for the attractiveness of its texture and appearance.

Clay

Clay can be bought cheaply from art shops or from most manufacturers of artists' materials. (Although, because it is heavy and postage expensive, it is sensible to wait until you happen to be going near an art shop).

Clay can be messy. Keep it in a polythene bag in a bucket with a lid to keep it from drying out. If it is going to stay unused for more than a few days, press a hole in each lump of clay and fill it with water. This will keep it moist and mouldable.

Before you let your child loose on clay-play the same kind of precautions as for painting are necessary. Cover the floor or table with newspaper and protect the child's clothes by putting on his overall. Produce the ever-useful tray and give him a 4″ cube of clay — a good satisfying weight to handle but not awkwardly heavy (don't forget

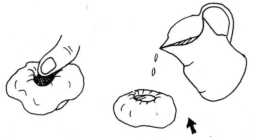

To store - indentations filled with water

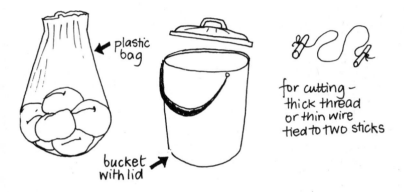

plastic bag

for cutting - thick thread or thin wire tied to two sticks

bucket with lid

that a 6″ cube is more than three times as heavy as a 4″ one). Show him how to 'wedge' it by throwing it hard onto the table — it makes a very satisfying bump.

At first he will be happy just to play with the lump of clay, feeling, squeezing and poking it. When he seems to want to move on from this give him a spoon, some lolly sticks, shells, buttons and similar objects that he can press into it. Later he will work the clay into recognizable shapes and objects: these you can leave to dry and then paint or varnish. Because they have not been fired and turned into pottery these objects are fragile, so it is unwise to fall in love with them.

Have a little dish of water for him to dip his fingers into. This keeps the clay wet and workable and can give it an interesting sticky texture. A piece of thick thread or fine wire is useful for slicing the clay.

Plasticine

This is very satisfying for modelling and has the advantage of not being messy like clay. Very young children enjoy cutting plasticine with their blunt scissors — it is much easier than cutting paper, in fact. This is good practice for them. Plasticine is ideal for making balls and snakes — it rolls out beautifully.

It is better to buy one large (one lb.) piece of one colour rather than the little strips of different colours that come with most sets. It can be bought at toyshops and art shops. Store plasticine in a covered container and don't use it on a polished surface.

Woodwork

You need not be afraid that small children will hurt themselves if you give them proper tools, and providing you keep a watchful eye on them. If they have a suitable table to work on and tools that are not too large for them, they will quickly master the skills of knocking in nails, sawing, drilling holes and turning screws. All this is excellent for their co-ordination and highly enjoyable into the bargain.

You need:

A firm bench or table   Not more than twenty inches high. You can cut down an old wooden kitchen table and nail battens across the legs to strengthen it or you can shape an old packing case into a rough table. If possible, fit a small vice to hold the wood while the child saws or hammers. If this is not possible screw wooden 'stops' to the corner of the bench — little wooden blocks about 2″ x 1″ which will keep the wood in place.

Tools   Buy the tools as you need them. This is usually better than buying a tool set which often contains inferior tools.

A saw   The best is called a 'gent's' saw and is, in fact, a small tenon saw.

Hammer   Not too heavy. A 4 oz head is quite enough. A joiner's tack hammer is ideal.

Nails   1″ and 1½″ wire nails, bought by weight.

Pincers   For pulling out nails

122

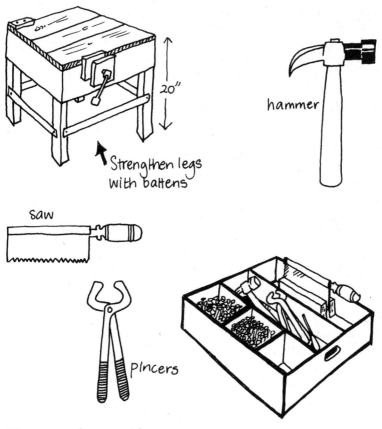

Glasspaper   for smoothing

Wood   Any scraps of soft wood will do. A do-it-yourself shop may let you have a free basketful from the waste sack. Orange-boxes, date-boxes and old wooden toys can be broken up to supply suitable wood.

As he gets more expert and enterprising you can add a small drill, a gimlet and a screwdriver and screws.

Storage   Keep the tools in a special box — an old cutlery box is ideal. Or Daddy might enjoy making a special little wooden box with clips and slots to fit the tools into. He will thus be able to carry his own tools around just like Daddy.

Cooking

There are a number of simple recipes that he can make by himself and others that require the minimum of supervision. If you have always encouraged a child to help you in the kitchen measuring and mixing will not be a mystery.

Fondants   8 oz icing sugar
               beaten egg white
               flavouring and colouring

Add the icing sugar to the egg white until it forms a stiff paste. Add a little colouring and peppermint essence if you like and shape into balls about three quarters of an inch in diameter. Flatten them. Fondant can be shaped into sugar mice with currants for eyes and a string tail. Add a little powdered chocolate to make chocolate fondant.

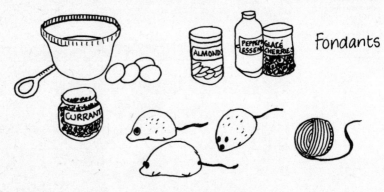

Fondants

Chocolate sweets   2 oz soft butter or margarine
                       1 oz chocolate powder

Mix together. Roll into balls. Roll in cocoa or hundreds and thousands.

Fairy cakes   1 egg
                  2 oz margarine
                  2 oz sugar

Mix well, then stir in flour and one small beaten egg. Shape into small cakes and cook for 20 minutes at Regulo 5 (350°). You can add chocolate chips, currants, cherries and other interesting goodies to this mixture.

124

Jam tarts
Probably the favourite. Give him some of your pastry, a rolling pin, cutter and patty tins. Let him spoon a little raspberry jam into each tart. Bake for 20 minutes at Gas Regulo 5.

Chocolate Krispies   2 oz bar plain chocolate
Rice Krispies or Cornflakes
paper bun cases
Melt the chocolate over a pan of hot water. Stir Krispies or Corn-flakes into melted chocolate. Spoon into cases. Leave to cool.

Flapjack   4 oz oats
2 oz melted margarine
1 dessertspoon syrup
Mix. Spread mixture in shallow baking tin. Cook 20 minutes at Regulo 5 (350°).

Chocolate crunch   1 cup self-raising flour
1 cup Cornflakes
1 cup coconut
1 tablespoon drinking chocolate
Add 5 oz melted margarine and mix. Spread in shallow baking tin and cook for 20 minutes at Regulo 4 (325°).

Bread
This is fascinating for him to help make. Let him stir in the yeast and sugar and see what happens and let him watch the loaf rise. Then let him knead the mixture and watch it grow again. Let him smell it as it bakes, see it as it comes out and taste the first warm and crusty slice.

Jelly
Melt the jelly in hot water in the usual way and pour into little cups or jelly moulds. Show him how to turn the jelly out by heating the mould a little in hot water before turning it upside down.

Instant whip
Pour the required quantity of milk into a bowl, add the whip mixture and mix with a wire whisk. Decorate with nuts, sugared almonds or cake decorations when set.
    Once he has been shown how to do it, he can carry on cooking by himself perfectly happily and with very little supervision.

Washing dolls and dolls' clothes

This marvellous game is best played on a sunny day out of doors, but if you are prepared to do a certain amount of mopping up it can be played indoors at any time.

You need a bowl of warm water, dish with soap, a flannel and towel. Place these in front of him and let him get on with it. At the end of the session you will almost certainly have to dry the dolls in an airing cupboard as water tends to get into dolls in a most surprising manner.

For the clothes add a little detergent or a few soap flakes to make plenty of bubbles. Have another bowl for rinsing and reserve a length of clothes-line or clothes-airer to let him dry his dolls' clothes.

Splash painting

Put three dabs of thick, different-coloured paint into three yoghurt cups. Put a small spoon in each. Fold a piece of plain paper in two, then open it up again. Dribble blobs of the different colours on one half of the paper, fold it shut and then press it all over. Open up and you have a beautiful pattern. This is always exciting because the pattern is always different. Thicken the paint with paste or flour so that it spreads but doesn't run.

Collage

This is any sort of picture made out of bits and pieces of material. You will need a paste such as Polycel (not heavy-duty Polycel), a brush and paper for backing. In the first instance show him how to tear coloured shapes out of, say, magazine advertisements, paste the backing paper all over and stick them on. Later he will sort out shapes and colours for himself and make recognizable patterns and pictures. At first, of course, he will merely plonk them on at random.

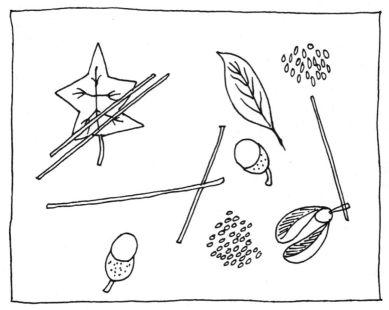

Snowman Cottonwool stuck on paper makes a splendid snowman who can be decorated with sticky paper or felt pen.

Cereal Make paste shapes on the backing paper and sprinkle oats, rice, lentils, macaroni, etc.

Fabric Cut up bits of various fabrics and stick them to the paper.

Leaves and flowers Dried leaves and flowers can be used to make some spectacular collages. You may need stronger glue.

Spice Sprinkle a little curry powder, nutmeg, cinnamon, etc., on the picture to make a fragrant picture.

Tissue paper This can be pasted flat and in several layers to achieve interesting colour effects. Or, when crumpled, it makes strange and exotic flowers.
All kinds of surprising materials can be used to make effective collages — milk bottle tops, sand, tinsel, postage stamps, shells, pebbles, matchsticks — use your imagination to help foster his. And not only flat backing paper need be used. Cartons and yoghurt cups make interesting objects to be decorated too.

128

Printing

This is a very satisfying activity for children of all ages. You need shallow dishes (plastic frozen meat containers are ideal) with a pad of absorbent material or sponge in the bottom. Pour a little mixed powder paint into each dish so that the pad is soaked in it.

There are now many things you can print with.

Potato Cut a suitably sized potato in half and use the cut half to print with. You can cut out patterns on this cut surface quite easily or nick the circumference to make pretty shapes.

Other vegetables and fruit Print with a cut carrot, onion, turnip, brussels sprout, apple.

Sticks and shapes Use the end of a pencil, the outside of a matchbox, cotton reel, sink plug, pastry cutter, child's brick, pieces of Lego, anything that will leave an interesting pattern when you print with it.

Raised patterns   Stick a piece of lace, sacking, corrugated paper, etc., to the end of a child's brick or cotton reel. This will always produce an interesting print.

Leaves   These are very effective. Press the underside of a leaf onto the coloured pad and print with this.

Hand   By now your hand (or your child's hand) is pretty messy, and you can try doing handprints. Press your hand onto the pad so that it is evenly coated with paint and use it to make handprints. It is fun to make a collection of family handprints.

Feet   If handprints are fun, footprints are even more fun. Have a bowl of clean soapy water ready for instant cleaning.
    Try printing on old pieces of sheet to make mats or dolls' blankets or curtains for a dolls'-house.
    Print on lining or wallpaper or the back of wallpaper and use it to paper the dolls'-house or Wendy house.
    Print all over the newspaper clothes (see page 155), to make them prettier and more realistic.

Sewing

Sewing cards   You will need a polystyrene tile and a thick blunt needle with wool knotted onto it. This makes a very satisfactory first sewing game as he pushes the needle through the tile.
    Once he is able to do this you can make your own sewing cards by drawing a picture on a piece of card and punching holes around the outline. Alternatively you can buy these sewing card sets in toyshops.

Simple animals   Cut two oval shapes from a scrap of loosely woven fabric (so that the needle goes through without too much effort) and let him sew them together round the edges. Use a thick needle and knot the wool to the eye (it is very frustrating to find your needle always unthreading itself) and sew the two pieces together. Let him leave a little gap and stuff the shape with bits of material, cottonwool or some other suitable stuffing. Stitch on a woollen tail and sew or stick on little bits of felt or buttons for eyes. Or you can draw them on with a felt pen. He has made a mouse or a cat or a dog... If you want to be really elaborate you can sew on bits of material for legs and ears.

Snake

Take an old nylon stocking or leg from an old pair of tights. He can stuff it with crumpled paper or rags and sew up the end. Then let him draw a face on it with a felt pen and sew on buttons for eyes. He will also have fun giving it an interesting body by drawing on it or by sewing on bits of scrap material. If very firmly stuffed these snakes make good draught excluders.

Junk

Collect a number of old cereal packets, cheese boxes, the tubes from toilet rolls and any other cardboard containers — anything that can easily be stuck together. Then show him how he can make constructions by simply sticking one to the other. At first he will enjoy the sheer fun of sticking things together but he will soon get the idea and produce some strange shapes of his own. Don't press him to name what he has made. The fun is in doing it and he may not know what it is. On the other hand he may well announce that it is a ship, an aeroplane, a house.

Leave his construction to dry and then let him paint it. It is very

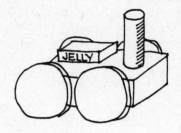

Boxes make all sorts of toys

important to find the right kind of glue that will stick these irregular objects and does not stain clothing or furniture. The PVA medium or Children's glue can be bought at big stationers or supermarkets.

Toilet roll tubes

Toilet roll tubes make all sorts of fascinating objects (they are, incidentally, quite safe. A manufacturer assured us that bacteria 'would be unlikely to survive in sufficient numbers to cause any harm').

Cut out one of the bell-like sections of a cardboard egg tray, stick it on the top of a roll, paint the whole thing red: a pillar box. Paint it blue, put a face on the front: a policeman. A face and cottonwool beard, paint it red: Santa Claus. A face on the front and a paper doily stuck round: an angel. Lay it on its side, stuff a ball of tissue paper in the end, draw a face on it, fringe a piece of brown paper and stick it over the tube: Dougall from 'Magic Roundabout'.

You can make impressive snakes and caterpillars from egg boxes. Round cheese boxes are useful as wheels and cotton reels as funnels or chimneys.

Sooner or later a child will try to use a toilet roll tube as a funnel for a train or chimney for a house or something similar. They are almost impossibly difficult to fix and this can result in an understandable fit of rage. Have a roll of Sellotape or a stapler handy and do it for him — one of the few instances where this is desirable.

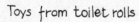
Toys from toilet rolls

Egg boxes which open longways can be fixed together easily

Pot of flowers

Get him to decorate a yoghurt cup with sticky coloured shapes or paste some pictures round the outside.

Give him some coloured tissue paper circles and paste them to the tops of wooden spills or paper drinking straws to make flowers. It takes quite a number of flowers to fill his flowerpot.

Pot of Flowers

Wax drawing

Show him how to make a drawing with white or yellow wax crayon on a piece of white paper. Now if he paints over it with not-too-thick paint, the paint will not adhere to the waxed parts and a magic picture will appear.

Sandpaper pictures

Put a piece of sandpaper face up under the white paper he is crayoning. It gives a most interesting bumpy texture to the picture he is drawing.

He can extend this activity by putting his drawing paper on other unusual surfaces — a wooden floor, a woven mat, a book or tray with an embossed surface. Later he can go in for bark, coal-hole covers, coins and other fascinating textures, but at this stage it is too difficult to hold the paper still enough.

Kites

'Proper' kites can be quite expensive and are really suitable for older children. But on a windy day an instant garden-size kite can be fun. Cut out a diamond shape from stiff paper or card and decorate it with potato prints or coloured sticky shapes. Knot pieces of coloured tissue paper onto a piece of thin string and tape or staple this to the point of the kite. Tie a longer piece of string to the other end of the kite and it should fly quite effectively. This kite won't last long, but you can always make another one the next windy day.

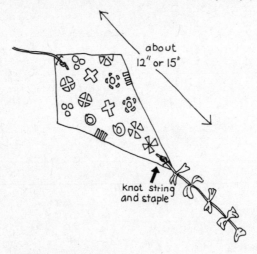

about 12" or 15"

knot string and staple

Chalks

Chalks are fun for a change. To be really effective they should be used on a dull black surface. This can be made by painting a flat piece of wood with blackboard paint. Let him wipe his own drawings off with a wet sponge or rag.

Geometrical patterns

Make for him some large geometric shapes in thick card and colour them brightly (use gummed paper or household paint). Make the basic shapes — square, triangle, circle, oblong, etc. — about four inches across. He can make these into all sorts of interesting shapes and patterns and he will also learn basic geometry from them. Shapes like these can also be bought.

Other toys he will love

A toy village, farm or zoo is always popular. The child can make his own setting with his own bricks and he will love to make the animals and people walk along the paths into their homes, pens or cages. The wooden peg toys that came with the wooden cars and trains will be invaluable now. You will be surprised at the way he improvises, talks to himself and makes up stories about his toys.

Cars and trains will also give great pleasure. You do not need an elaborate layout, but a bridge of some kind is fun. Show him how to build one with his own bricks and a small strip of wood. A good idea is to draw a road layout on a large piece of card or hardboard and let him use this as the base for some of his games. It can be stored behind a piece of furniture when not in use.

Matching games, sorting games, jigsaws

Matching games of any kind are excellent for pre-school children. They train the eye to recognize similarities so that when your child begins to read the shapes of individual letters are much more quickly assimilated. The same goes for sorting games and simple jigsaws. Remember that he will need a vocabulary to describe the similarities and differences he is identifying. So talk to him and discuss what he is doing.

Puppets

Puppets that are strong enough and simple enough for children to work themselves are helpful at this stage. Simplest of all is a paper bag that fits over the child's hand and on which he paints a face and hat. Slightly more complicated is a sock covering the hand. Tuck the toe into the palm, hold the fist horizontal, with the thumb as the lower lip. Two bits of felt or sticky labels form the eyes.

Sock puppet

tuck toe of sock between fingers and thumb

Paper bag puppet

The terrible crocodile   This is huge fun, though too complicated for small children to make for themselves. You need a pair of socks. Cut the entire foot from one and sew it onto a cut you make opposite the heel of the other. This forms the jaws of the beast. Cut two pieces of stiff cardboard the length of these jaws and insert into each jaw (this is for rigidity when small fingers and thumbs cannot reach the ends of the socks). Decorate with button eyes and cardboard or matchstick teeth and then insert the hand, fingers into upper jaw, thumb into lower. This fearsome saurian is the obvious basis for some riveting stories.

Body for puppets   The simple shape of a puppet dress with openings for head and two arms (two fingers and thumb) can be sewn by the child himself if the material is soft and loosely woven and if he has a big blunt needle (tapestry needle) with wool knotted onto it. The sides and shoulders are stitched but, of course, the bottom and the other openings left open. The ends of the sleeves can be gathered and cardboard or felt hands stuck or sewn on.

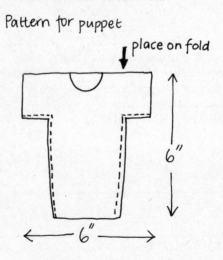

136

Heads of puppets: 'Squeezy Lemon'. These plastic lemon-juice containers can make convincing puppet heads. Make a hole at one end or in the middle, depending on whether you want a long or a flat head. Make it big enough to get a finger comfortably in. Use strong glue to stick on wool for hair and eyebrows, cottonwool for beards, etc. Make the features from coloured sticky paper or bits of felt.

Toilet roll tube: cut this in half and stuff the inside with newspaper so that it sits firmly on the finger. Matchsticks are useful for noses, pushed into holes pierced with knitting needles. Buttons will make the eyes and a hat can be made from a circle of sticky paper cut along a radius and gently folded.

A tennis ball or other small rubber ball with a hole cut in it for the index finger will serve as the basis for a puppet head. So will a lump of plasticine. A lump of clay, formed when wet and shaped round the finger, can be left to dry out and then painted. This is effective but rather fragile.

A cotton dish-mop makes a woolly-haired puppet on a stick. Either tie all the ends together to form a face onto which buttons or bits of felt can be stuck or push the stick through a plastic lemon so that the mop forms the hair.

Puppet heads

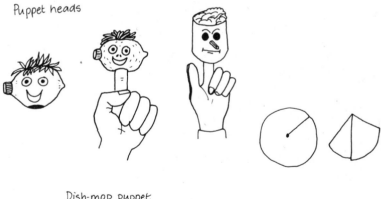

Dish-mop puppet

Small boxes like Smartie or jelly boxes that just slip over the hand can be painted to make simple puppet heads. Wool or cottonwool can be stuck on for hair.

Flannel-graphs

These are easy to make and very popular. Cover a square of cardboard or plywood with a piece of material with a slight pile — corduroy, velvet or felt are ideal. Cut out attractive pictures from Christmas or birthday cards or something similar, stick little pieces of the same material that covers the board to the back of them and you will find they will cling to the board quite easily (the principle of the commercial 'Fuzzy Felt' sets is the same). Children can now make up their own composite pictures and the stories to go with them. Big geometric shapes are often useful for making interesting patterns.

Flannel graph

← flannel stretched over board

cut-out pictures with bit of flannel on the back

Papier mâché

Most small children find making papier mache fun but if their interest flags be prepared to carry on by yourself until they can decorate the finished product. You will need newspaper and paste — lots of both.

Tear the newspaper into small pieces about 1″ x 1½″. You will find newspaper tears more easily in one direction than another. Put the pieces into a bucket of water to soak thoroughly.

These pieces of wet paper and the paste are the basic materials. From them the child can construct a host of interesting objects.

138

Pots and pans Grease the outside of a yoghurt cup or the underside of a plastic plate. Lay a layer of the wet pieces of paper all over this greased surface. Put paste all over the paper and lay another layer of pieces of wet paper. Continue this process until you have six or seven layers evenly pasted on.

Leave to dry for a few days. When thoroughly dry it will come away from the greased surface quite easily, taking the shape of the mould. When trimmed it can be painted and varnished.

Mask Blow up a round balloon until it is the size of a child's head. Grease the surface and, as with the pots and plates, lay on a layer of wet pieces of paper and carry on until there are six or seven layers. You can make a nose by 'bandaging' on a lump of squeezed-out paper. Leave it to dry. Then prick it to burst the balloon inside. You can cut eye and mouth holes in the dry mask, make a big hole in the base and use it as a helmet. Or you can carefully cut it in half and use it for *two* masks.

Papier mâché can be squeezed into countless shapes and used to form all kinds of animals, puppet heads and models. Always 'bandage' more sizeable models with strips of paper and paste and don't be too disappointed if they crumble to pieces when they dry out completely.

Mask

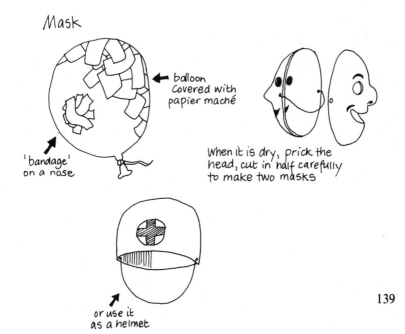

balloon
covered with
papier mâché

'bandage'
on a nose

When it is dry, prick the
head, cut in half carefully
to make two masks

or use it
as a helmet

139

Cereal box shops

You need a cereal box with the top cut off and an old mail order catalogue or piles of magazines with lots of pictures and advertisements. Cut round two sides of the front of the cereal box and hinge it open. Draw lines across the inside of the box and the exposed surface of the front to make 'shelves'. Let the child cut out pictures from the catalogue or magazines and stick them onto the shelves. In this way it is quite easy to construct a complete street of shops — grocer, shoe shop, toy shop, dress shop, etc.

Shop

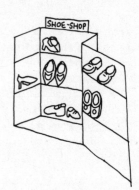

Cereal box fish tank

Cut the front completely off a cereal box. Paint the inside of the box a greeny-blue to look like the sea. Get the child to colour and decorate fish shapes cut from stiff card and attach these to cotton threads with Sellotape. Put the box on its side and suspend these fishes from under the other side. Cover the front with cellophane paper and you have a fine aquarium.

Fish tank

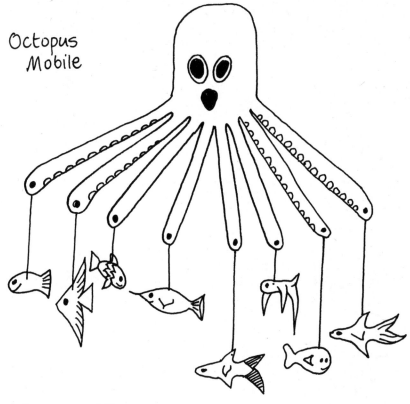

Octopus Mobile

Octopus mobile

Cut out an octopus in stiff card. Cut out eight fish shapes in card and colour them with crayons or scraps of coloured paper or cellophane. Attach them with a thread of black cotton to each tentacle. Add another thread to the head of the octopus and attach it to the ceiling. Our daughter made us one long ago and it is still swimming majestically from the ceiling of our living-room.

10 Playing With Other Children

For the first three years of their lives or so, small children are happiest and busiest playing by themselves. So long as Mother is nearby to give reassurance and security, his own company and that of his toys and playthings is all he needs. If two or more small children are put together at this stage, they are quite uninterested in each other and play individually without any attempt to share each other's toys. Indeed, if one small child takes a liking to another's rattle he will crawl over and take it, and provided the second child is immediately given something else to play with, he will be quite unconcerned.

By the time a child begins to walk he will also begin to notice other people, although he will only respond properly to his family or to other people he has seen often and knows well. But he will still not be prepared to socialize with other children because he is still unable to see them as other individual human beings. Many mothers are alarmed when they see their toddler deliberately hitting another child and then watching its reaction of rage and fear. Similarly if he himself is attacked he will react in the same way but be incapable of hitting back. This is nothing to be alarmed about. The fact is that the hitter is unable to understand what he is doing: to him the crying child is another interesting variety of squeaky toy. He cannot understand the connection between causing and feeling pain just as he cannot communicate properly.

How then does he begin to socialize with other children? How does he learn to share his toys and co-operate in playing games? Firstly, of course, he learns a great deal by imitation. As soon as he is able to walk he will, for instance, want to 'help' his mother or father in whatever they are doing. This will be followed by a phase when he copies his mother or father exactly, taking over their role completely as he scolds his dolls or talks to his teddy. This discovery of personal relationships by actually becoming someone else marks an important stage in his development.

With the growth of his vocabulary, moreover, he discovers that he can make things happen. He says 'milk' and he is given a mug of milk. He says 'ball gone' and someone helps him find it under the sofa. As his grasp of language improves his sense of frustration increases, because he simultaneously discovers that he cannot make everything work his way. Hence sudden uncontrollable tantrums.

With this growing awareness of himself and his own capabilities he also becomes aware of other children, though in a very primitive way. He will quite happily play the same game as another child — digging sand in the sandpit, pushing toy cars along a track — but if he decides he wants the other child's spade he will grab it. This can have two possible results: if he succeeds in getting the spade away the other child will howl, but not try to grab it back. If he does not succeed both will keep hold of it and howl until an adult separates them.

Imperceptibly this snatch-and-grab stage merges into one when he first becomes willing to share. He will, of course, still grab for things for a long time to come, but less and less frequently. Equally, he will be prepared to share more and more often. This is largely a consequence of his increased vocabulary and understanding. If he can talk about sharing or waiting his turn he can begin to co-operate and be patient. This ability to share and co-operate grows quickly and within a few months he will have completely accepted the necessity of taking turns if the game is to be any fun.

This new-found ability to play happily with other children will necessarily mean that he comes into conflict with them less often, although anyone who has dealt with small children knows that occasional squabbles are inevitable. But children actively enjoy co-operating — climbing the climbing frame together, taking turns to go down the slide, building a joint sandcastle. They also cease to be too possessive: they will push their cars round their sandcastle together without one of them saying, 'This is *my* sandcastle! Take your car off *my* sandcastle.'

A favourite game is playing mummies and daddies, cooking imaginary cakes together, and taking it in turns to pour out imaginary tea. A sign of having arrived at the social stage is two children collaborating to do a jigsaw.

As children near school age they are able to take an even more relaxed view of sharing. They will be able to play board games like snakes and ladders or wait for their turn in a family game of pelmanism (see page 183). They will also be able to take on specific characters in their games of Mummy and Daddy and be prepared to obey the orders of other children. The cowboys and Indians will have leaders and hunt together in groups.

It is not until children have been at school for two or three years that they are able to work together properly as a team rather than as a group of individuals. This progress can be clearly charted. The typical two-year-old wants a ball all to himself and will cry if it is taken away from him. The typical three-year-old will trust an adult to return a ball to him when he throws it, but not a contemporary. The four to five-year-old will enjoy running after a ball and trying to kick it into a goal or picking it up to throw again. But the idea of working as a team and passing the ball to one other to be kicked, hit or thrown comes only after several years of contact with contemporaries at school.

For this whole essential socializing process to take place properly it is important that the child should mix with other children as early and as often as possible. After the age of about three it is even more important, and the child who is isolated from his contemporaries can easily become introverted. The importance of nurseries and playgroups in this connection can hardly be overstated.

It is important to remember, however, that the child needs introducing gently into a new social environment. It is not good enough to dump a child among a bunch of strangers and leave him there for two or three hours to play. Most children are frightened and bewildered by new surroundings and the noise and bustle of a group of children. It is imperative that a mother should give her child confidence by staying with him until he has come to terms with his new surroundings. When he has he will be quite content to let his mother go and soon he will not give her a glance when she leaves him.

This chapter is concerned with ideas for groups of children playing together. Naturally, many of the ideas in earlier chapters can be adapted, but older children will soon demand something more stimulating and imaginative. Finally, most of the ideas here are ideal for the highly demanding business of giving a small children's party. The sensible thing is not to expect them to understand organized games apart from the very simplest.

144

Dens

All children love dens and will make them out of anything anywhere — behind the settee, in a large packing-case, under the table, among the Michaelmas daisies or inside an elderberry tree. Others go so far as grabbing a spade and beginning the unrewarding task of digging a hideout; fortunately while the enthusiasm is high the digging is easy. When the digging gets tough and enthusiasm begins to flag discreet parents can suggest a construction over the top of the hole made of boxes, planks and old curtains or blankets so that there is somewhere to play in.

You may occasionally be lucky enough to get some sizeable pieces of old cardboard: in default of these cardboard boxes from your grocer will do. Open them up and flatten them out so that you have big flat pieces to build with.

With the aid of Sellotape or liberal amounts of glue or staples you can now build an enormous rocket or submarine. Cut round peep-holes for windows or make holes so that you can stick toilet roll tubes into them: these make good periscopes or observation ports. Make other holes with a pencil and stick wheels and knobs from one of the construction toys into them to make controls that they can manipulate. Let the children paint or decorate it themselves, with stuck-on pictures, crayons or felt pens. Making a den is enormous fun and it really doesn't matter that this kind of den is not very durable: when it finally disintegrates this is a splendid excuse for building a new and different one.

Den ideas will normally come from the children themselves, but if nothing emerges you can often encourage them to produce something by starting a conversation about hospitals, Red Indians, firemen, witches or something similarly provocative.

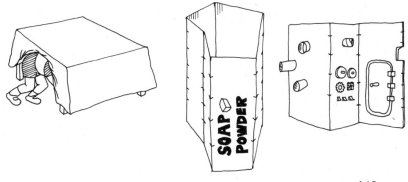

Hospitals

These have been mentioned before in Chapter eight. With a little ingenuity a considerable 'surgical' battery can be built up — strips of old sheet for bandages, little bottles of water for medicine. A cot mattress or eiderdown forms a bed. Most loved of all, of course, is a stethoscope, and plastic toy stethoscopes can be bought at most toy shops. They make an excellent present for children at this stage.

Red Indians

If you have an old sheet or curtain, abandon it to the children and let them paint pictures over it with lots of bright poster colours or powder paints. It can then be made into a very effective tent in a number of simple ways: indoors by putting a broom over two chairs, outdoors by tying three canes together and draping it over them. A totem pole can be made by sticking cereal boxes together into a tower six feet high and painting faces on them. Do this and let them dry before assembling them. Red Indian hats are fun and easy to make (page 152). A pretend campfire can be made by taking a piece of board or a tray, piling a few sticks on it and pushing red and yellow tissue paper between them.

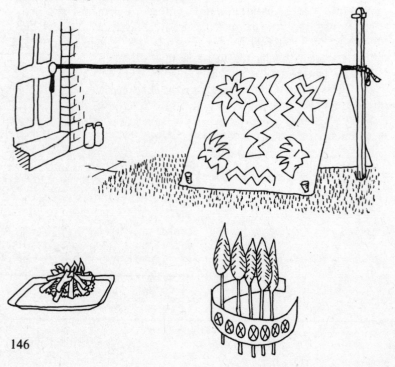

Best of all is a real camp fire under adult supervision in the garden. Children love to collect twigs and sticks for this and will enjoy poking it with a long stick from a safe distance; this is your responsibility. By your attitude you can teach them a valuable lesson about fire — not being terrified of it but treating it with continual respect. Make the point about not playing with boxes of matches.

If you wrap potatoes in kitchen foil they will cook beautifully in the ashes of a fire. Some case-hardened fathers will prefer to cook them without the foil, just like scout camp all those years ago. Apples wrapped in foil cook more quickly and are delicious — if very hot. Sausages on sticks remain firm favourites.

Firemen

Any construction will turn itself into a fire-engine provided it has some kind of steering-wheel to turn; the round lid of a tin will do and it doesn't have to be attached to anything. A stepladder, bunk ladder or anything that can safely be climbed makes a fireman's ladder and a piece of hose (you don't need water) completes the illusion. An impressive fireman's hat can be made from folded newspaper.

Witches

Children love scary games and witches are especially good because they can wear masks, hats and dressing-up clothes, as well as painting their faces. A 'gingerbread' house is a splendid idea. They can make one by taking a large cardboard box or sticking together two or three egg-packing boxes from the grocer. Decorate the outside with painted pictures of cakes and sweets or any food pictures cut from magazines and catalogues. This makes a fine den for the witch

147

to hide in. When the children tire of this game the den can be adapted for something else.

Wendy house

The 'home corner' has been described before (page 107), but now is the right time to check its contents and to add to them. There is no nned to buy special — and expensive — children's furniture because improvisation is simple and the children themselves will help you produce all the necessary items, which is much more fun anyway.

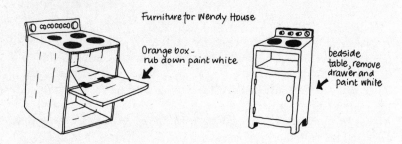

Furniture for Wendy House

Orange box - rub down paint white

bedside table, remove drawer and paint white

Cooker Use an orange box — greengrocers are usually quite glad to get rid of them, especially if you say what you want them for. Smooth it down with sandpaper and paint it white. Stand it on end and paint four black circles for cooking rings on the top. Nail a strip of wood across and add cotton reels and other small round objects as knobs and dials. Attach a piece of wood to the middle shelf by two hinges so that the oven door will flap open and fix two pieces of string to the door and the box so that the door will open down to the horizontal.

You may be lucky enough to see a bedside table in a junk shop. This also makes a convincing cooker if painted in the same way as the orange box. Remove the drawer, and the bottom cupboard now becomes the oven. Paint cooking rings and add knobs and dials as for the orange box.

Furniture Junk shops and jumble sales are treasure houses for finding all sorts of useful equipment for the home corner provided it is clean and safe. For example a wooden drawer can be converted into a table or a bed by the addition of four wooden legs. Screw them to the inside of the drawer for the table, to the outside for the bed.

148

Table - made from upturned drawer

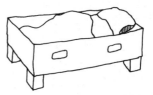
Bed - made from large drawer

The home corner should have a table, a chair or stool, a cooker, a bed for dolls (or preferably for the child himself — a large drawer with a little bedding will do) and shelves for putting treasures on. Small equipment might include pastry cutters, dustpan and brush, telephone, a tea set and plenty of pieces of material for tablecloths, dusters, bedding, and so on.

Dressing up

This has been discussed on page 107, but here are some more suggestions.

Jumble sales are good places for finding clean discarded clothes which are ideal for the dressing-up box. Look out for oddities like frilly waist slips and bridesmaids' or party dresses — these will be much admired and worn for a large number of roles. A skirt can be floor length on a child. Net curtains make effective bridal veils: sew on a little elastic so that they stay put on the child's head. Old hats often get stuffed away in the backs of wardrobes. A little attention will usually revive them. Hats with big brims or flower hats are favourites. Old shoes, especially glittery or dressy shoes, fascinate

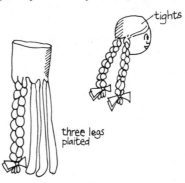
tights

three legs plaited

149

children and they love to clomp around in them. Old handbags are useful for carrying an amazing variety of objects about in.

Toy hats — policeman, postman, fireman — are assets for children's games or fantasies. If you're lucky enough to know someone in the business, an old postman's hat or a building worker's plastic helmet are pure magic.

Make a wig from a pair of tights, plus the four extra legs from two other pairs of tights. Tie two extra legs to the top of each leg of the original tights and make two plaits. Tie a ribbon at the end of each plait.

But perhaps the most fun of all is being allowed to try on Mummy's clothes and necklaces and use her make-up — just for a very special treat when the children are having a very special game.

Shops

Everything needed to make a splendid shop can be found right in the home — packets, tins, jars, fruit and vegetables — all the usual things that the housewife shops for. The contents of the larder (where suitable) and the cleaning cupboard (when safe) plus shopping baskets, paper bags, purse and real money make the perfect combination. If your kitchen scales can stand it, they could be included in the game.

At this age children do not need telling how they should do it. They have seen their mother shop and will use this experience. All they will usually do is to exchange goods for arbitrary sums of money. They will talk real amounts — five pence, twenty pence, two pounds, etc., and wil give and take change, but don't expect them to get their sums even remotely right. This game can go on for some time and at the end, when everything is sold, all the goods can be put back on the table, the roles of housewife and shopkeeper reversed and the game started again.

They buying and selling of little cakes that the children are then allowed to eat can be an occasional exciting variation.

A useful extension of 'shops' is to allow the child a few pence to buy something of his own choice at the local shop. Equally, most children are thrilled to be allowed to ask the bus conductor for the tickets.

Assault course

All small children like to show off their physical prowess and constantly test their physical skill. This is why they are continually climbing, balancing, clambering and crawling, pushing and pulling, jumping and rolling. Children of this age will have already held their balance while walking along a plank and crawled through a cardboard-box tunnel. You can join these activities together to make an 'assault course'. This should be moderately difficult for them and your imagination will soon suggest some interesting variations. Upturned tins can act as stepping-stones so that their feet do not touch the floor. A ladder from a bunk bed or a pair of steps laid between two chairs makes an interesting obstacle. Jumping off a chair onto a cushion is also fun. The only limitation on an 'assault course' is that it should be safe, i.e., it should be testing but not dangerous. Chairs tip up very easily.

If you have a garden you can add other hazards such as a strawberry net to crawl under, an old tyre to clamber through or a hosepipe on the ground to walk along. A tree, of course, offers many opportunities — a rope to swing from, a tyre on a rope as a permanent swing, a rope ladder, a 'nest'. A climbing frame, slides or permanent swing — or a combination of all three — is a perpetual source of pleasure. If you are unable to have one yourself there is nearly always a children's playground within walking distance that the child can be taken to. To climb the big slide is very confidence-building. Playgroups and nursery schools almost always provide apparatus of this kind.

If — as sometimes happens — a group of children do not want to play with any of the toys or games you offer them and you have reasons for not wanting them racing noisily from room to room, here are some suggestions.

Things to make

Crown

You'll need: paper plates; crepe paper; coloured tissue paper; paste; stapler.

Draw a zigzag line down the middle of the paper, cut this and you

Crowns

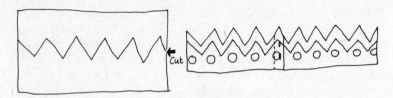

have material for two crowns. The children can decorate these with paints, paper shapes, or potato prints or any other colourful and convenient material. When they are completed they can be stapled to fit their creators' heads. If you cannot find pieces of paper as large as this take a sheet from a wallpaper pattern book and join the two halves together with staples.

Red Indian headdress

You'll need: strips of corrugated cardboard 1″ x 20″; paper feathers (cut from stiff wallpaper); drinking straws; crayons, coloured sticky shapes, etc., for decoration; staples, Polycel or Sellotape.

Give each child its strip of corrugated cardboard. This is to be decorated much as the crown. Cut feather shapes about 6″ long and 1″ wide in stiff wallpaper and let the child decorate these with crayons etc. Stick the decorated feathers to drinking straws and insert these in the holes of the corrugated cardboard strip. Staple or tape to fit the maker's head.

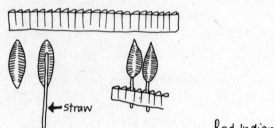

Red Indian Headdress

Easter bonnets

You'll need: paper plates; crepe paper; coloured tissue paper; paste; stapler.

152

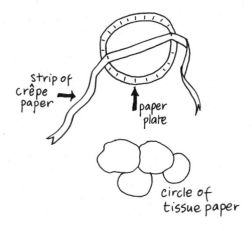

Strip of crêpe paper →

paper plate

circle of tissue paper

Easter bonnet

Cut the tissue paper into circles or squares about 3" across. Cut the crepe paper into long strips about 1" wide and 36" long.

Give each child a plate, a crepe strip and an assortment of tissue paper squares or circles. Staple the strip of crepe across the underside of the plate so that the ends hang down evenly on either side. The children can now decorate the top side of the plate with tissue paper flowers. It is then ready to wear, prettily tied under the chin.

Helmets

You'll need: large sheets of stiffish paper approximately 23" long (the width is immaterial as the wider the paper the greater number of helmets that can be cut); crayons, coloured sticky shapes or printing equipment; stapler.

Fold the paper in half. Draw hat shapes from the fold outwards — imagination will suggest crowns, Roman helmets, postmen's caps, jesters' hats, etc. Cut the shapes out, let the children decorate them, then staple to fit the children's heads.

It is sensible to practise making helmets with sheets of newspaper before embarking on the real thing.

Helmets

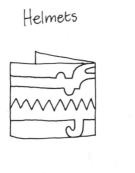

153

Masks

You'll need: cereal boxes; paints, sticky coloured shapes, etc; elastic; stapler.

Cut the cereal boxes in half along the narrow sides. Each half then makes one mask. Cut holes in the front to correspond with the child's eyes, nose and mouth (adults can be helpful here). Let the child paint or decorate the mask. Staple the elastic to the sides of the mask to go round the child's head to hold the mask on.

Cottonwool makes good hair or beard. Strands of wool make effective hair or eyebrows. Tissue paper can be used to make a hat to go on the top of the mask.

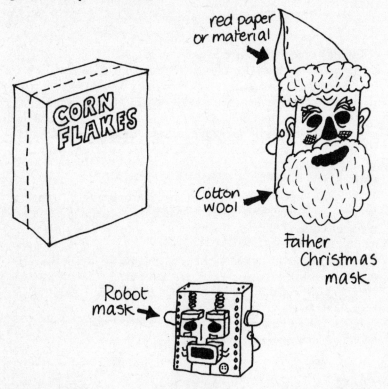

Paper mats

You'll need: squares of paper 12″ x 8″; paints or decorations; scissors.

Paper mats make good presents for small children to give

154

favoured adults or to use themselves. Let them fold the paper in half several times and snip into the corners and sides of the folded paper. This gives an interesting appearance when opened up. The mat can now be suitably decorated. Old Christmas cards, pictures from magazines, coloured sticky shapes or potato printing etc. can all be used to good effect.

Newspaper clothes
You'll need: piles of newspapers; wax crayons; decorations — paints, sticky shapes, etc; scissors.

Let the children take it in turns to lie down on sheets of newspaper to have various garments drawn round them with the wax crayons — jumper, skirt, trousers, etc. These can be cut out and decorated by the owner. The resulting garment can then be variously used — hung on a clothes-line across the room, Sellotaped to the owner, etc.

Necklaces
You'll need: macaroni (big size); milk bottle tops; cardboard discs; wool; large blunt needles (tapestry).

It is always fun to make and wear your own necklace and practically anything that can be threaded onto wool with a large blunt needle will do — bits from construction toys, pierced acorns and conkers (a job for adults), buttons, etc.

Knot a needle to a length of wool or wrap Sellotape round the end of a piece of thin string, secure a piece of macaroni to the other end so that the 'beads' won't fall off and let the children thread their own necklaces.

Games to play
There are several simple games that young children can play without too much organizing. At this age the traditional 'Oranges and Lemons' and 'Nuts in May' are still a little too complicated, so it is sensible not to try them yet.

Touch game
Put interestingly shaped objects into cloth bags and get the children to guess what they are by feeling them through the cloth.

Ask the children to sit on the floor and let them come up in turn to guess. Always take the object out of the bag afterwards to show them whether they were right or wrong.

155

Suggestions Spoon, apple, banana, book, egg-whisk, toast-rack, pastry cutter, hairbrush, screwdriver, rolling pin, teacup, key, etc.

Kim's game (simple version)

Put six objects or so onto a tray and let the children sit round and look at them. Now cover the tray with a cloth and remove an object as you lift it off again. The children guess what has been taken away.

Some interesting variations of this game suggest themselves, e.g., one of the objects is always replaced by a new object. Or the children guess in turn.

Musical bumps

A favourite with all young children. Put a record on and let the children dance to it. When you stop the music they must all drop onto their bottoms on the floor. They will be prepared to do simply this for some time, but after a while the last child to reach the floor can be 'out' until only one is left. At this age children do not have much of a competitive spirit and aren't really interested in your picking a winner so don't make a big thing of this.

This game can be varied by getting the children to climb onto something when the music stops. Or just lie down.

What have you got in your shop today?

You need room to move and a fertile imagination for this game. The children come to you and chant together 'What have you got in your shop today?' You reply, 'Bouncing balls,' 'Walky-talky dolls', 'Talking parrots', 'rabbits', 'tigers', or anything else you can think of. The children then go and act the part until you tell them to stop. Then they return to you and chant for another subject.

Acting nursery rhymes

Many nursery rhymes lend themselves to acting and children often enjoy dressing up and playing 'Little Miss Muffet', 'Humpty Dumpty', etc. Only the very simplest props are necessary and the children can take turns in the star role. Abandon this game quickly if they lose interest.

Please Mr Crocodile

Someone is appointed Mr Crocodile. He sits in the middle of the floor with all the children one side. They chant, 'Please, Mr Crocodile, may we cross your golden river,' and he replies, 'Only if you have fair hair', 'Only if you have red trousers', 'Only if you have black shoes', or something similar until all the children are across.

Mulberry bush

A very old favourite. Your great-great-great-grandmother knew it was old in her time. Hold hands in a ring, skip or walk round and sing. Suit the actions to the words.

> Here we go round the mulberry bush
> The mulberry bush, the mulberry bush
> Here we go round the mulberry bush
> On a cold and frosty morning.

> This is the way we wash our hands
> Wash our hands, wash our hands
> This is the way we wash our hands
> On a cold and frosty morning.

Then hold hands and start again. 'Clean our teeth', 'Sweep the floor', 'Clap our hands' are familiar, but variations are easy to invent.

The farmer's in his den

Another old and interminable favourite. Someone is chosen to be the farmer and the rest form a ring, holding hands around him. They walk round him singing:

> The farmer's in his den
> The farmer's in his den
> Hey ho the dairy-oh
> The farmer's in his den.

> The farmer wants a wife
> The farmer wants a wife
> Hey ho the dairy oh
> The farmer wants a wife.

At this point the farmer chooses a wife who joins him in the middle.

> The wife wants a child, etc.

She chooses a child who also joins them.

> The child wants a nurse, etc.
> The nurse wants a dog, etc.

157

The last verse is:

> We all pat the dog, etc.

This hilarious episode is normally followed by the dog becoming the next farmer.

Hokey-Cokey

If you don't mind lots of noise, let them all join in a hokey-cokey. This always goes down particularly well at the end of a party and everyone joins in. The actions, obviously, follow the words. The tune is traditional. Stand in a circle.

> You put your right hand in
> You put your right hand out
> In, out, in, out,
> Shake it all about
> You do the hokey-cokey ... [shake the body]
> ... and you turn around
> That's what it's all about.

> Oh, hokey-hokey-cokey [all hold hands and rush to the centre]
> Oh, hokey-hokey-cokey [reverse previous action]
> Oh, hokey-hokey-cokey [first action]
> Knees bend, arms stretch
> Rah, Rah, Rah! [clap hands three times].

> You put your left hand in, etc.
> You put your right foot in, etc.
> You put your left foot in, etc.
> You put your whole self in, etc.

A few hints on running a party for small children. Think of lots of things to do beforehand and prepare them carefully. It is a good idea to let the young guests loose among your children's toys for a little while first. Have dressing-up clothes, bricks, trains and large cardboard boxes around. Then settle them down to making their own party hat to wear at tea-time. Cut enough crown or hat shapes beforehand, have the pieces ready, together with paste and stapler, and newspaper to cover the floor. Many of the things mentioned in this chapter can be adapted for a party with musical bumps a firm favourite, and if you feel courageous enough a flannel-graph story or a story with finger puppets will calm them down afterwards. Try playing shadow pictures.

Have all the food and drink for tea prepared. Best of all have it already laid in a separate room before the first little guest arrives. Don't forget that these days children prefer savoury cocktail sausages to sticky cakes and jam sandwiches. Give them sausages on sticks, nuts, crisps, cubes of cheese, raisins, Smarties, paste or Marmite sandwich fingers, chocolate and iced biscuits. If you provide a birthday cake they may well enjoy the candles more than the cake itself so be prepared to wrap slices of cake up for them to take home. Squash is the ideal party drink. Ice cream is a universal favourite.

Try to get another adult to help you. You can often work this with another mother on a You-help-me-I'll-help-you basis. She can help clear up, take children to the lavatory, etc.

Children love a tiny present when they leave. Wrap it up, name it and let them rummage for it in a large box. Tins of bubble-blowing mixture, tubes of Smarties, balloons, little books. And, of course, they can take home all the hats, mats and masks they have made at the party.

11 Those Endless Questions

From the very first weeks of a baby's life he begins to become aware of change and variety — change of temperature, wetness and dryness, light and dark, hunger and comfort. Gradually he begins to compare and categorize these experiences and, as he develops, he discovers that they all have names. At first he does not question anything he sees or experiences: indeed he does not have the vocabulary to do so. But the experiments he carries out continually prove and confirm things to him. He repeats an action until he establishes a definite concept, a real understanding of what he is 'playing' with.

The first questions a child asks are really concerned with the sheer power of language — 'Wassat?' He names familiar objects and finds out that what he says has meaning and can be understood. A dog is a 'doggie' and a horse a 'big doggie' until he is able to recognize and categorize and subdivide brown four-legged animals into 'dog' and !horse'.

And once he can put coherent sentences together he starts to ask 'Why?' and 'How?' Quite often these questions have a quite different meaning from the surface meaning. They are testing that the communication system is still working properly — that every question *does* have an answer. The accuracy of the answer is quite immaterial as, often, is the content of the question. But at some time during these pre-school years his curiosity about the world he lives in develops suddenly and then adults are subjected to an impossible barrage of questions. The quest for knowledge is irrepressible. What makes the thunder? What is glass made of? Why is the sky blue? How do I grow? What happens when I laugh? What does it feel like when you're dead?

There is no obvious way that questions like this ought to be answered. So much depends on the question itself, the knowledge and articulateness of the adult, and his general attitude towards children. This, of course, may be coloured by how he himself was answered when he was a small child.

Often it is best to talk around the question. Where a specific answer is, for one reason or another, impossible, a short lecture on, say, climate, biological growth, glassmaking, is usually enough. Detail is not very important. As long as the child gets a general idea that is all that is necessary. The child has been reassured that his question does have an answer and he will retain what he finds useful to him.

At this stage of their development children are like blotting paper, able to absorb dozens of new facts and experiences every day. What is important is not so much the value of this new information but the acquisition of words to describe and explain it. Now, in fact, is the time when the child really builds his working vocabulary. This is why it is vital that he should be talked to, listened to, talked to, talked to, talked to. It is the only way he will learn.

Books now begin to become really important, especially if you yourself are weak in areas that the child finds interesting. These areas will necessarily vary according to location, social location, and the feelings of the parents themselves. There are several series of simple reference books — the 'Observer' books spring to mind — that are useful sources and well illustrated. A second-hand encyclopaedia can be a godsend, although adults are warned against encyclopaedia salesmen who can persuade unwary people that an expensive encyclopaedia is necessary if the child is to survive in the competitive world of today. Not so! We ourselves find a pre-First World War set of the Everyman Encyclopaedia an invaluable source of basic information. And there are many excellent children's reference books on the market such as the Macdonald Starters which cover most topics simply and clearly.

But with the best will in the world, there will still be questions quite impossible to answer immediately. The answer here is to say *something,* even if it is only 'Well, I don't really know, but ...' The vital thing is not to discourage further questions. If a child is constantly told to 'Be quiet' or 'Stop asking questions' or 'Leave me alone' or [1]'For God's sake give me a little peace', he will begin to think that his natural curiosity is somehow wrong. If this happens he may withdraw inside himself and by the time he begins school the real damage will have been done. He will have formed his defences and learned to be docile or aggressive, but not lively and curious. Here are some suggestions as to how this essential natural curiosity can be developed and fostered.

Nature

How plants grow

Line the inside of a glass jam jar with blotting paper. Slip a few dried peas or beans (horticultural, not larder, variety) between the paper and glass. Put an inch or two of water into the jar and keep it topped up. Soon the roots will reach down and the shoot climb up.

Suspend a potato an inch or so over a jar of water. It will soon produce roots and shoots.

Cut off the top of a carrot or turnip — as in normal preparation of vegetables for cooking — and put it in a saucer with a little water. The leaves soon begin to sprout and flourish.

Put an onion — or other bulb — over the neck of a narrow jar filled with water. The roots will grow rapidly and fill the jar.

An exotic example: pierce an avocado stone with three holes into which matchsticks are inserted and suspend the stone (blunt end downwards) over a jar of water so that the base just touches the surface. It will produce a spectacular display of root and shoot.

Many of the fruits the child eats can be persuaded to produce shoots — lemon and orange pips, date-stones, chestnuts, etc.

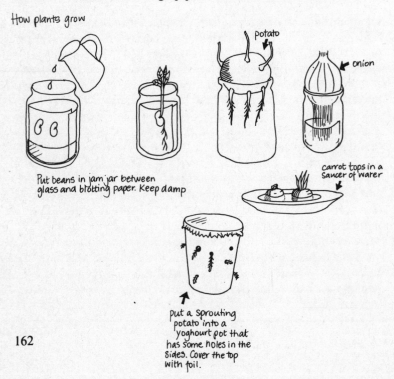

How plants grow

Put beans in jam jar between glass and blotting paper. Keep damp

potato

onion

carrot tops in a saucer of water

put a sprouting potato into a yoghourt pot that has some holes in the sides. Cover the top with foil.

Plants need light

Put a little square of tissue into two small dishes and sprinkle a few cress seeds on each. Keep the tissue damp. Put one dish in a dark cupboard, the other on the window sill. See which grows quicker.

Plants need light

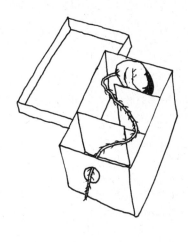

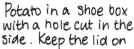

Potato in a shoe box
with a hole cut in the
side. Keep the lid on

Potato in a shoe-box   Put a potato that is beginning to sprout into a shoe-box with a lid and a little hole cut in one end. Look at the potato each day and see how it grows towards the light. A fascinating variation of this is to put a couple of strips of card into the box which successively block off the light from the shoot. The shoot will zig-zag its way round and past them.

Cress ball   Cut a marrow in half lengthways and scoop out the inside, leaving about half an inch thickness of rind. Prick the rind through with a skewer or nail. Sprinkle cress seeds (or grass seeds) inside the two halves, close the marrow up again — you can Sellotape the two halves together — and hang it up where the child can see the cress grow through the holes.

You can make a similar cress ball with an orange or grapefruit. Scoop out the flesh, make holes in the skin, sprinkle with seeds, fill with earth (keep this damp) and watch the cress come through.

163

Cress ball

 ① Cress seeds in plate. Keep damp.

 ② Make holes in grapefruit skin

 ③ Cover with the half grapefruit

Plants need water

Take three jam jars and put a piece of crumpled cloth in each. Sprinkle with cress seeds. Half fill the first jar with water, slightly moisten the second and leave the third dry. The results will be a graphic demonstration of a basic fact of nature!

Cut a piece of celery. Put it into a jar of water with a little vegetable colouring. Next day cut the celery across and see the coloured spots where the celery has 'drunk' the water.

Helping in the garden

If you are lucky enough to have a garden, one of the most fascinating things a child can do is to help plant seeds or seedlings and watch them grow. At this stage it is sometimes tempting to offer them a patch of their own. This will be enthusiastically accepted but do not expect a small child to become a dedicated gardener overnight. Don't be disappointed if he neglects it, forgets about it or just abandons it. The joys of gardening are essentially adult. On the other hand his own personal plant — tomato, bean, marrow, etc. — will be lovingly tended and its produce proudly harvested and eaten.

No flat is too small for a little window box where a few fast-growing plants can be sown, watered and observed.

Small children are naturally interested in playing with earth and should be encouraged to do so. Making mud pies is always an absorbing game and it teaches them about the properties of earth and water.

A spadeful of earth

Dig out a spadeful of earth and put it into a large bowl or tub. Let the child explore it, pull it apart with a trowel or large spoon and discover all the variety of things in it — living creatures, seeds, roots, stones, debris, etc. Explain to him — as far as you can — what everything is and let him get to know the complexity of what he is walking around on.

Replace the spadeful carefully — and let him see you do it.

Wormery

For this you need a fair-sized glass jar two-thirds full of soil into which you introduce a few large worms. Keep the soil damp but not wet; cover it with a layer of sand and on top of this a layer of old wet leaves. Put brown paper around the jar and put it in a cool place for about a week.

When you remove the paper to show the child what has happened you will see that the worms have made a pattern through the layers, demonstrating clearly how they turn the soil over. Don't forget to replace the worms in the garden afterwards.

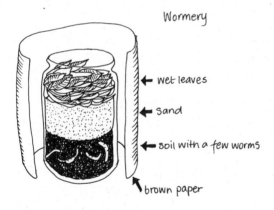

Wormery

← wet leaves

← sand

← soil with a few worms

↖ brown paper

The undersides of stones, rocks and logs

Show the child what happens when you lift up a stone, rock or log. Let him observe the creatures that live in this damp, dark environment. Replace the stone carefully.

Do the same thing when you are out for a walk in the country and see the different varieties of creature. Repeat this wherever convenient: it fosters a child's natural curiosity and interest in nature.

The seaside, of course, is ideal for making this experiment in a different context. When the tide is out, rockpools, the underside of stones and just scratching around in the tidal sand will reveal dozens of fascinating little creatures. An illustrated guide is more than useful. As with garden stones, replace all seaside stones carefully.

The major point being made here is that it is important to expose the child to the natural world. Urban children tend to miss a great deal — the noises and smells of the countryside, the cycle of the seasons, the lore that goes with close contact with the earth. As far as it is possible they should be given this contact, with a sympathetic adult to explain, to demonstrate, to discover with. It can pay rich dividends in later life.

The weather

Changes in the weather are evident to all small children and they can soon learn a great deal about the world they live in by observing and describing them. Evaporation can be demonstrated by putting a saucer of water on the window-sill and finding that it disappears. Condensation can be shown by putting a cold plate in the steam from a kettle. Dripping bathroom windows make the same point, and of course they are ideal for drawing on.

A rain gauge

A straight-sided jam jar or plastic beaker makes a perfect rain gauge. Put it in the garden or on an outside window-sill, flat roof, etc., and measure how much rain has fallen in any one day, week or individual rainstorm.

Temperature

If you can afford it, invest in a maximum-minimum thermometer (this measures the highest and lowest temperature over any given period). It is great fun to inspect it each day to see how hot or cold it was the previous day. You can easily plot the temperature on a graph by spacing days along the bottom of a piece of squared paper and temperatures down the side and recording highest and lowest temperatures by means of red and blue lines respectively. A small child will quickly grow to understand what you are doing together and things

min. max.

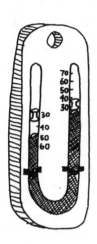

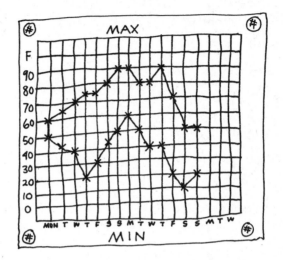

like snow, a really hot day or a sudden chill in summer will take on a
new significance.

Weather chart

This, of course, can be connected with the temperature chart. Rule
lines a fair distance apart on a piece of paper to make biggish
squares, say 2″ x 2″. These, horizontally, represent the days of the
week. Put the date in the corner and let the child colour in a represen-
tation of the previous day's weather in each square — a yellow sun
for sunshine, a blue umbrella for rain, an outline snowman for snow,
etc. Or, of course, you can cut out large numbers of symbols from
coloured sticky paper. This progression of symbols day by day and
week by week helps children grasp the meaning of 'tomorrow' and of
things that are going to happen in the future.

Weather chart

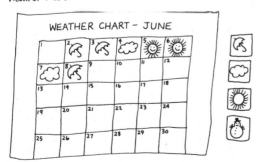

167

Time

Small children learn about time in a number of ways — from the way they see you fill in your dairy, the way the family uses the *Radio Times* and *TV Times,* the way that certain things happen on certain days. This sense of time, the logic of events happening in a predictable sequence, is important to their understanding of their surroundings.

Birthday calendar

Family, or classmates', birthdays are exciting events to small children and a birthday calendar is a good way of maintaining this interest.

You need six pieces of card or stiff paper about 8″ x 8″. Each side represents a month and is appropriately labelled. A vertical line down the middle of the card and sixteen horizontal lines across give each month enough days. Now fill in all the family birthdays. Punch two holes at the top of each card, thread a piece of string through and hang the cards up where they can easily be seen. They can be decorated with pictures cut from old birthday cards and so on.

As family birthdays come up, the child can see them approaching day by day and join in the excitement of it all.

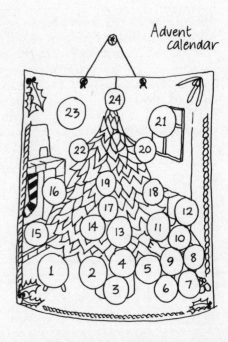

Advent calendar

Advent calendar

Find an old Christmas illustration or Christmas card (not too small) with plenty of interesting detail. Buy a packet of sticky-back labels and number them from one to twenty-four. Stick them all over the picture to cover interesting details. Punch two holes in the top of the picture and hang it up where it can be reached easily. Start on 1 December and pull the relevant label off each day and see the picture gradually emerge. You can of course buy advent calendars and these are fun too.

Light

A sundial

Let the child discover for himself that a compass always points in the same direction, i.e., the needle always points to the same place in the room. Then let him see that the sun always rises and sets in the same place. Now you can make him his own sundial. You'll need the compass and a stick about a foot long. You will also need a sunny day. Push the stick into the ground so that it stands vertically. Let him see what happens to the shadow of the stick hour by hour, and mark its changing position with small sticks. He will find that the sundial still works perfectly the next and every sunny day.

Shadows

Once a child is conscious of his own shadow it will fascinate him. It will do so even more so if you show him how to use it. There are many shadow games you can play with him from simple chase games involving trying to tread on each other's shadows to quite complex games trying to make his shadow 'go' somewhere.

Shadow pictures Fix a table lamp so that it shines brightly on a wall and make funny shapes with your hands. Living creatures are popular and a little practice will enable you to make beautiful butterflies, giraffes, horses, cows, dogs and cats. Your own brand of mythical beasts can be hilarious too and the child will certainly want to join in — so encourage him.

An interesting variation on this is to have a sheet across a room with a table lamp behind it. If you then stand between the lamp and the sheet your shadow will be projected clearly onto it. You can dance, wave your arms about or otherwise make interesting movements. Or you can perform certain actions and get your friends to guess what you are doing. This is fun at a children's party, letting everyone have a turn.

Shadow pictures

Maps

If his parents drive a car a child may be familiar with maps. Show him how they work and identify the features you are going to come across — bridges, churches, forests, windmills. If nearly all the driving is in town show him where you live on the street map and point out where you are going and how you are going to get there. Tell him, again, what you expect to see and let him discover the places for himself. Make a game of this — who is going to see the church, the traffic lights, the Town Hall first.

Teach him to be observant by making him look closely at things he takes for granted on familiar journeys, e.g., to the shops, to a friend's house, to the park. Look for different things each time — the colour of gateposts and front door, the different kinds of dogs and cats, the trees, the flowers, the lamp-posts, the letter-boxes.

Manholes

All children are interested in holes in the road. Workmen will usually tell young children what it's all about — drains, gas, electricity, telephones. This can be taken a stage further by counting the various manhole covers in the road and working out what they are there for and what part they play in the home. Manhole covers in pavements, incidentally, make excellent rubbings. A large sheet of paper and a wax crayon will produce decorative results and are quite easy for children to do.

Mirror

Even the smallest mirror can produce some odd effects. Stand an ordinary rectangular handbag mirror on the page of a picture book, move it around and see what happens. Do the same with other familiar objects. Mirrors are fun too for reflecting little spots of light that can be chased, or spotlighting different objects.

Kaleidoscope

Kaleidoscopes are not expensive to buy, but even so it is fun for your child to help make one of his own. You need two long narrow mirrors of the same length. Hinge them together with Sellotape down the long edges. Cut a piece of card the same size as the mirrors and tape this to the two free edges of the mirrors, making a triangular tube, mirror-sides in. Close the bottom with some translucent material — coloured cellophane, tissue paper or the like — and now drop a few small, brightly coloured objects — beads, buttons, sequins — down the tube and look down. You will see a pretty pattern which you can continually change by shaking the kaleidoscope.

Periscope

A simple periscope is easy to make. You need two small mirrors, a ruler and some plasticine. One mirror is fixed at each end of the ruler with a piece of plasticine, so that they face each other at an angle of something like 45° — experiment will show you. You will find you can see round corners with it.

Coloured spectacles

Make a pair of spectacles out of cardboard and stick coloured cellophane, such as toffee paper, over the eyeholes. When these are worn common objects will take on a new and interesting appearance.

Magnets

Magnets are mysterious objects and can provide the basis for a great many activities. Make sure they are not too fiddly and that you have a supply of interesting iron objects — nails, screws, small toys, etc. A pair of bar magnets are also quite easily obtained and the 'push-pull' effect is fascinating for a child to experiment with.

Fishing game   Cut some fish shapes out of stiff paper and let your child colour them or otherwise decorate them on both sides. Fix a paper clip or a bent pin on each fish's mouth. Tie a small magnet to the end of a pencil with a piece of string or cotton — and go fishing!

Magic paperclips   Put a paperclip on a piece of stiff paper held flat and hold a magnet underneath it. Make the clip move about by moving the magnet. Let the child work this 'magic' by himself.

How things work

All small children like taking complicated things to pieces. Slowly and with total concentration they will dismantle an old clock or gramophone motor and it seems to be one of the things that can hold their attention for hours at a time. It is the same with some adults.

So if you have an old clock or any similar piece of superfluous machinery, give it to him with a small screwdriver and let him get on with it. A word of caution here: make sure he does not realize that it is a clock mechanism. If it is very obviously a clock you may find that he later dismantles the priceless Swiss masterpiece on your mantelpiece. Do not let him dismantle electrical equipment.

Electric light circuit

This is not to say that he won't find electricity interesting. But let it be on the proper scale. Fix him his own electric circuit by taking a piece of softboard and fixing to it a 3-volt battery, a 2½-volt light bulb in a bulb-holder, some bell wire and a switch. Any schoolboy will show you how to wire it. The child can then switch the light on and off whenever he wants to. A bell or buzzer circuit works in exactly the same way.

Electric light circuit

Locks and keys

A collection of locks — and keys which fit — can provide a very absorbing pastime. Keep them together in their own box and he will fit the keys to the right locks over and over again. If he wants to see how a lock works, by all means provide him with a screwdriver. But don't expect the lock ever to work again.

Sound

Different objects, or similar objects of different sizes, produce different sounds. This can be demonstrated in a number of ways. Make your own banjo with a shoebox and elastic bands. Cut a hole in the lid about three inches across and put large elastic bands right round the box and across the hole (to give resonance to any sound produced). You can shorten the elastic band by pressing down on it with your finger. When plucked the bands will therefore make sounds of different pitch.

A length of narrow copper pipe (the kind they use in modern central heating systems), cut to different lengths and hung up to be struck with a spoon or a stick, makes excellent chime bars.

Jars or bottles (milk bottles are good) filled with different levels of water sound different when tapped with a stick or spoon. By judicious pouring and adjusting a set of 'bottle bells' can be arranged which will produce recognizable tunes.

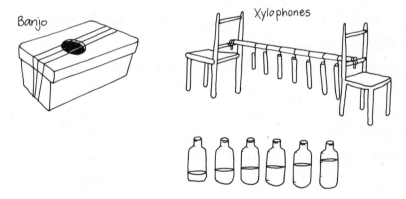

Banjo

Xylophones

Telephone

You can make a simple and effective children's telephone with string and two yoghurt cartons or something similar (make quite sure there

173

telephone

are no sharp edges). Make a hole in the bottom of each, thread the ends of the string through, and knot so that the cups are firmly attached. Let the child have one cup and then walk away until the string is taut. If the child puts the cup over his ear and you whisper into your 'mouthpiece' distinctly, he will hear you quite clearly, and vice versa.

Water

By the time a child reaches the age of three he will know a great deal about water. In fact, one of his very earliest memories is that of being bathed. But there are many other interesting properties of water that he has not come across and which can teach him about how the world functions. For instance, he can empty a full bucket of water into an empty one by siphoning water out of it through a length of plastic or rubber tube. He will see that the water stops flowing when water in the two buckets reaches the same level. How curious — and how instructive! And how about the effect that air pressure has on water? A transparent plastic beaker in the bath will show that water will not flow into it when it is inverted however hard you push it down. On the other hand water will not flow out of an inverted tumbler until air is let in.

Water can make things turn too. A plastic water-wheel is cheap to buy and when put under a slow-running tap it is fascinating to see the little plastic buckets fill with water and push the wheel round. A water-wheel like this can be used with dry sand as well.

Pets

Children love animals and some kind of pet in the home is good for teaching children about life — and death. Moreover, a pet is something a child can talk to and be comforted by when the world is difficult and adults are behaving badly. Pets can also introduce children quite naturally to the facts of birth: the excitement and joy at the prospect and then the appearance of puppies, kittens or even white mice has to be seen to be believed. Grief at the death of a beloved pet is not a bad thing either. It is a necessary preparation for inevitable greater bereavements later in life.

174

Care must be taken that protection works both ways: that the pet does not bite and isn't likely to frighten the child and conversely that it will not itself be damaged by over-affectionate handling. Luckily both children and their chosen favourites usually show considerable resilience: anyone who has seen a three-year-old confidently stuffing its arm into the maw of a huge dog will come away with new respect for the tolerance the animal kingdom often shows for mankind.

Dogs and cats

Too much is known about these splendid domestic animals for any further rehearsal here. In the rare event that you don't know how to train and handle one, there are countless books to help you.

Guinea pigs

If you have room for a cage, guinea-pigs make attractive pets, practically odourless unless badly neglected. Another advantage is that their babies are born perfectly formed and can be handled — gently — almost immediately. Guinea pigs rarely bite and get used to being handled by small children very quickly.

Hamsters

These are easy to keep, but the fact that they are nocturnal creatures presents difficulties: they tend to sleep when the children are awake and to go in for violent and noisy activity when the parents are watching television. Fascinating because of the enormous amount of food they can stuff into their cheek pouches, but they have been known to bite the hand that feeds them and also to eat each other.

Gerbils

These engaging little creatures used to be known as desert rats. They breed easily (some say too easily) and are active during the day.

Rabbits

They make ideal pets but normally need a great deal more room than they are allowed. Ideally they should have a fair-sized lawn to graze and exercise on.

Tortoises

Not ideal pets in the British climate and most imported ones die a miserable death at the approach of winter. Only if you are really prepared to look after it should you let your child have one of these remarkable reptiles as a pet.

Goldfish

Simple to keep. Avoid goldfish bowls which act as lenses and are cruel to the fish, and keep them in a proper aquarium.

Pond life

If you have a chance to go pond-fishing a day's work with net and jam jar can yield rich results. Nets are also cheap and almost universally available but if you cannot buy one a good substitute can be made from the foot of an old stocking attached to the top of a bamboo pole with a circle of stout wire. Every kind of pollywog can be caught and identified through a reference book, before putting them back in the pond.

A trip to a pond in February will often produce frogspawn. Don't take too much — frogs are getting scarcer — but enough to let the child experience the wonder of developing tadpoles. And don't forget to return the baby frogs to the vicinity of the pond. It is cruel to let them loose in suburban gardens where their only path to water is across lethal main roads.

Birds

Some people like caged birds, some object very strongly to them. But certainly the behaviour of wild birds is more interesting than that of caged birds and the variety infinitely greater. You can attract them by putting crumbs and stale bread out and perhaps the most attractive way of doing this is to build a bird table. If you live in a flat you can make one by extending a flat piece of wood out from a window-sill. Don't forget that birds need water as well as food.

Bird pudding

This is attractive to all birds. Mix pieces of bread, cake, grains of corn, nuts and pieces of apple in a cup with some melted lard and put the mixture into the fridge. When set, turn out from the mould, put it into the kind of net oranges are sold in and suspend it where birds can get at it. It will not go unnoticed for long. Again, a reference book is useful to identify the various birds that visit you.

12 Ready for School

In his fifth year your child will be admitted to 'big school', that land-mark in his life that he has been looking forward to for some time because it means that in his eyes he is at last grown-up. But the step forward is often accompanied by anxiety on the part of both parents and children, particularly in the case of an eldest or only child.

First is the question of scale. Even a small school is a great deal larger than anything the child has been used to, and with many more and larger children. Corridors are long, rooms are large, and instead of one loving and concerned adult there seem to be a number of remote and unconcerned adults. He must adjust to this new state of affairs. All the evidence shows that he will do so much more quickly and easily if he has already played and mixed with other children, especially at playgroup or nursery school. This, in effect, is a power-ful plea for parents to see that he does just that. However loving his home environment may be, it will not protect him from the size, the noisiness, the sheer scale of his first school.

The second problem is one of discipline. It is not that infant schools are rigidly regimented — quite the reverse — they all provide a cheerful and relaxed environment for small children. Nevertheless, the problems involved in handling thirty or more small children demand that certain new rules have to be learned and obeyed. He must learn to stand in line on certain occasions, to be quiet when the teacher is telling a story, and not rush down the corridor. He must hang his coat up on the same peg every day and learn to share and take his turn. All these things, and many more, give a new order to his life. If he is self-confident and outgoing he will very soon learn to accept these odd new rules cheerfully and wholeheartedly. He will want to please his teacher and he will be pleased if she is pleased with him.

Another new factor is the introduction of competitiveness into his life. Before now he has enjoyed playing games for their own sake and winning or losing has been incidental to the pleasure of playing them. But now, with many more children around, he will find the need to assert himself, to establish his identity among them. Just as the 'I am *me*' stage establishes him in his family, this '*I* am important too' stage is a sign that he wants and needs to establish himself in this new and more complex situation. The wish can take many forms, perhaps the commonest being a phase of extreme boastfulness. 'My daddy has a great big blue car.' 'Well, my daddy has two big cars — bigger than a house.' Parents should not interfere with this or try to stop it with ridicule. It will pass when he works out his place in the new hierarchy and realizes that his identity as an individual is not threatened.

Then — and this is something few parents ever realize — there is a difference in toilet habits. Before now, going to the lavatory was a private affair, with familiar arrangements of seat and flushing and with plenty of toilet paper. Suddenly all this is changed. Instead of the little room at the top of the stairs there is a row of lavatories with noisy children banging doors and possibly peering over the top. The lavatories themselves may be some way from the classroom, or across a large and rain-swept playground, and often there is no toilet paper — the children have to ask for it from the teacher beforehand. These are formidable circumstances for a small child and constipation or, occasionally, soiled underwear are not surprising. There is, alas, no easy answer to this problem. Generations of educational and psychological neglect are not going to be solved by a couple of angry parents demanding better treatment for their child. Yet certain things can be done. The parents can discreetly acquaint themselves with the school's toilet arrangements, encourage their child to go to the lavatory before school and put a small personal supply of familiar paper into a trouser or smock pocket.

Finally a child learns that the world is not always kind. Before now when he has been thwarted there has usually been some reason for it and his resulting tantrum has in a way evened things out. But now he will begin to learn that virtue is not always rewarded and that fate can be quite arbitrary in how she dispenses her favours. Usually the first signs of this, and of the child's strong disapproval of this state of affairs, is that adults hear him say, 'But that's not fair.' His sense of natural justice is being outraged and he is recording his protest. He *knows* what is fair and it will take him a few years to work out that fairness is not always the criterion. 'It's not his turn.' 'He's got more than me.' 'I'm older than her, so I should go first'. These are signs that the child is coming to terms with the environment he will have to exist in as an adult.

The problems parents face are necessarily wider: how is my child going to get on? Will he be happy? Will he fit in? What's the teacher like? All these reflect the worries of parents who are letting their fledgeling out of the nest for the first time.

The problem is greatly lessened if the child has attended a play-group or nursery school or, at very least, mixed with a lot of other children. Children who have learned to play happily with others, and who have also learned that the absence of Mother does not mean the disappearance of Mother, will settle in much more quickly and easily. Their cheerful demeanour and desire to get back to school as quickly as possible are more reassuring than any words.

A further problem that worries many parents is what appears to be a sudden lack of communication between themselves and their child. 'What did you do at school today?' 'Nothing!' Why, the parent wonders, doesn't he want to tell me about all the new things I *know* he must be doing. The answer has little to do with withdrawal. Quite simply, he has found himself in a situation that he has not yet acquired the vocabulary to describe. So 'nothing' is the nearest he can get to it. If a parent needs reassuring on this point, ask the child what he had for lunch!

The final problem for most parents is the highly charged one of reading. Should they or should they not encourage their child to read before he goes to school? There have been many lengthy answers to this question and books have been written about it, but in our view the answer is 'don't push it' — time enough when he gets to school, particularly if you have given him all the preparation that he needs and is described here. By this we mean that there comes to every child a time when he reaches 'reading readiness' and little you can do will hasten this. By trying too hard and making him feel guilty about the whole subject you could even retard it. Once your child is ready to read he will show signs of wanting it. Of course, you will notice this more quickly if you have been in the habit of talking and reading to your child. After all, he cannot show you that he is ready to read unless he has the means to do so. This is why we have stressed again and again the necessity of talking to a child, giving him mastery of the language, giving him a vocabulary that allows him to explore the world and to develop his curiosity.

The way he uses this vocabulary is a reflection of this essential curiosity. His inquisitiveness and experimentation throughout his early years have given him the opportunity to reason, to compare and then to choose the right words to fit his thoughts and actions. And all the things he has been given to play with have stimulated his senses and increased his ability to manipulate his environment. Eventually this leads him to accept the abstract concepts of word and number that are going to dominate his early years at school.

This last chapter is specifically concerned with those things that can ease the transition between home and school. In one sense all the preceding chapters have been about this, but the suggestions made here deal mainly with how the child can be familiarized with letters, words and numbers in all their various forms and combinations.

Picking out symbols

The beginnings of formally learning to read are fraught with difficulties that most adults have mercifully forgotten. It is for instance no problem for an adult to distinguish between 'boy' and 'dog'. To an inexperienced five-year-old they can look fearfully alike. 'This' and 'that' can appear only minutely different to the untrained eye. So it is important that small children are treated with the utmost understanding and sympathy on the nursery slopes of literacy.

It is not easy. Moreover there are snares. 'I know what that spells,' says one bright four-year-old, seeing the word 'Esso' — 'Garage'. And indeed, the infant world is full of things with name-shapes he grows to recognize through sheer familiarity — 'HOOVER', 'CORN-FLAKES', 'TV TIMES', 'HEINZ' and so on. But when he goes to school, of course, he may come across lower case letters for the first time and find that all the symbols have different shapes from those he is used to. It puzzles him.

'What is that letter?' he asks, pointing to an 'H'. What do you reply — 'aitch' or 'huh'? And never forget that you and his school may have completely different ideas about how to teach reading.

These scattered points are not assembled to depress you, merely to show you the complexity of the problem. How, then, can you help? In round terms, anything that helps him recognize shapes helps.

Matching pictures

This is something an adult and a child can make together. Cut out of magazines, catalogues or other expendable material identical pictures and stick them onto cards. These can be used for all kinds of matching games, for sorting games and for 'Pelmanism'.

Picture Dominoes

Happy Families

Pelmanism

This is a very good game for children of all ages and, incidentally, one that even very young children can become good at. It requires a pack of cards with similar or identical pictures on them. Snap cards, Happy Family cards or even your own home-made cards (see above) will do. All you have to be sure of is that there are two or four of each picture.

Place the cards face down on the table. Take turns to turn over two cards. If they match, you keep them and have another go and so on until you fail to pick up a matching pair. If they don't match, you turn them face down again. The idea is to remember where the cards are when it comes to your turn so that you yourself can match them if you or a player before turns up one of them. Children get very quick at this and it is an excellent method of encouraging them to remember shapes and pictures. Ordinary playing cards can, of course, be used, but for small children it is sensible to remove the sixes, sevens, eights, nines and tens.

Playing cards

Playing cards can be used for a number of sorting and matching games. Leave him to play with them by himself. He will probably sort out colour and suits but numbers will usually be recognized more on pattern than on a numerical basis. Nevertheless it is a good introduction to numbers.

Picture dominoes

These can be bought or made. Cut strong card into twenty 2″ x 4″ strips. Colour each end a different colour, using four or five different colours in various pairs. The game is to match the colour by laying the cards out end to end, red to red, green to green and so on. Other things can be substituted for colour, of course — paper mosaics, flowers, patterns and any kind of matching picture. Ordinary dominoes can be introduced when the child is able to count rather than recognize by pattern.

Happy families

Easy to make, and children like to help. Cut out a series of 'family' pictures — dogs, girls, cars, houses, prams, shoes etc. — and stick them onto cards you have previously coloured so there is a set of pictures on each set of coloured cards. Write 'Blue' at the top of the blue cards and 'Dog' or whatever the appropriate picture is at the bottom.

Another way of doing it is to take a mail order catalogue or something similar and cut out a slightly more complicated set of 'families', e.g., things that go into different rooms. The kitchen set would include cooking utensils, the living-room chairs, television, sofa, etc. A large picture of each room would also be stuck down on a card. The small cards would then be turned face downwards and the children would see who could complete their room first.

There are many imaginative variations on this game and children themselves are not slow to make creative suggestions.

Scrapbooks

Decorators sometimes have obsolete wallpaper books which can be turned into excellent scrapbooks. Take four or five sheets and staple or sew them together. Make several of these books so that your child can keep each set of pictures separate, e.g., babies, football, flowers. Stick one picture on the cover of each and write 'football' or 'flowers' underneath. On a wet day or when appropriate take them out and go to work with scissors and paste on a pile of old magazines. When the child becomes bored, put them away for another rainy day.

Writing own name

Long before he can read or write properly, it is a good idea — and very good for his morale — if he can recognize and write his own name. Do this with a capital initial letter followed by lower case letters — John, Jane, Susan. When he goes to playgroup or nursery school, these interesting symbols will be printed by his cloakroom peg, etc., and he will recognize them immediately.

Keeping toys tidy

It is useful to keep small toys in individual boxes or plastic containers clearly labelled. He will soon learn to recognize both picture and word as symbolizing what is inside — 'cow jigsaw puzzle', 'building bricks', etc.

Pencils, crayons, paint, paper

The desirability of having these materials handy for the child to use has already been stressed a number of times. He should know where the tin in which the pencils are stored is, and where there is some paper. If pads are too expensive, paper bags and used envelopes can be opened up; children are not critical and will willingly use any surface that can be drawn or painted on. Ingenious parents can always find a way of acquiring cheap drawing paper, whether it is a local printer who will give away offcuts or a friend in an office who has a source of ancient memos printed on one side only. The important thing is that if the child wants to draw or colour, he should be able to do so. The fact that he is familiar with these fundamental creative processes will, incidentally, help him a great deal in his new school where they are universally encouraged.

Sorting

These are two types of sorting: 'structured' and 'unstructured'. In 'unstructured' sorting the material to be sorted is without pattern — like the jar on the mantelpiece where you put odd buttons, paper clips, drawing-pins and pieces of string because you cannot think of the proper place to put them at the moment. In 'structured' sorting the material can be categorized — like the contents of a cutlery drawer which can be sorted into knives, forks and spoons. Both can be very rewarding: unstructured because of the excitement of wondering what you are going to find next and structured because it gives the child a sense of achievement. Laying the table or putting away the crockery are both forms of 'structured' sorting as he 'helps' around the house. It is possible to buy games based on structured sorting into colour, shape and size, but any house contains enough material for dozens of sorting games like this — buttons, coins, cotton reels, etc.

In an earlier chapter we suggested that geometric shapes should be given to children and that these should be added to from time to time. This was to enable the child to experience differences in size, shape, texture, etc. Sorting these out in various ways will continue to give a child a great deal of pleasure.

Form board

On page 27 we recommended that the geometric shapes should be cut out of a piece of plywood and that the remaining piece should be saved. Now is the right time to take this piece of plywood and mount it onto another piece of plywood of exactly the same shape and size, well sanded and painted. Put knobs on the geometrical shapes originally cut out for easy handling and let him fit them into the holes in the board. If he quickly finds this too easy, cut the geometrical shapes into two pieces with a knob on each.

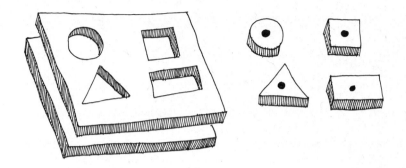

Counting

From about the age of two 'counting' has been largely a matter of matching — one for me, one for you, one for him, etc. Typical would be laying the table — a spoon for Daddy, a spoon for Mummy, a spoon for Nicky. The child finds this understandable in a way that an abstract list of numbers — 1,2,3,4 — is not. He literally cannot imagine a number being divorced from a thing — a number as a symbol is meaningless to him.

Nevertheless, children love to count and should be encouraged to do so — how many spoons, how many stairs, how many buttons, how many fingers. In this way they will be able to cope with numbers successfully long before they are able to understand the numerical symbols.

'Number words'

These are words which enable the child to express ideas of quantity — wide, big, short, full, more, thick, tall, etc. They are, of course, all relative. Our elder daughter, for example, was taken to the zoo when she was four years old. She was astonished at the huge size of the elephant and when, later, we were looking at the big bird-eating spiders, she demanded to know what was so interesting. 'Big spiders.' 'I want to see!' With some trepidation we lifted her up. She looked at them and said impatiently, 'No, no, I want to see the *big* spider!' Indeed, size is relative. But it is important that children can handle ideas of quantity easily and much of their early play is about this.

Weighing can indicate 'more' or 'less', 'heavy' and 'light', 'a lot' or 'a little', 'large' or 'small', 'larger than', 'more than', etc.

Measuring can indicate 'long' or 'short', 'tall', 'little', 'wide', 'narrow', 'thick', 'thin', 'thicker than', etc.

Water play can indicate 'empty', 'full', 'more' or 'less', 'nearly empty', 'almost full', etc.

Peg-board

It is worth investing in a peg-board and a bag of pegs. Or one can be made from special peg hardboard. Stick two sheets together over a sheet of plain hardboard, making sure the holes are aligned. Make sure these are 10 x 10 holes because pegs to fit come in hundreds with ten pegs of ten different colours. At the beginning children will stick pegs in at random, but after a while they will sort the pegs out carefully and put them in lines or make patterns with them.

A good idea is to make two peg-boards, then make your own patterns and get the child to copy them, gradually making the patterns more complicated. This kind of imitation will not stunt the child's creative imagination: it is a challenge to his hand-eye co-ordination. Of course he will make up his own patterns at other times.

When he starts school you will probably find that he uses a similar board as part of his counting training. If he wants to count this way encourage him without forcing him.

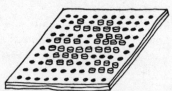

Bingo

Although number symbols do not mean much to him, he will enjoy a game of bingo with his brothers and sisters or other children. This is, in effect, picture lotto, but using numbers rather than illustrations. Let him play by himself, making a simplified board and numbers on the discs to match.

Dice games

Make a simple board game by drawing a road and dividing it into a couple of dozen squares. Draw a 'character' — a cat, an elf, a child — at the beginning and a 'home' — a den, a house, a tent — at the end. Take a cube building block and make spots on its side, but *not* more than four. Two can play taking turns to throw the dice to see who gets home first.

Whose birthday?

Divide a piece of card 12″ x 8″ into four vertical columns and draw a birthday cake at the top of each column. Make twelve circles in each column, each the size of a 2p piece and coloured differently in every column. Have ready a collection of counters coloured like the columns. Throw dice and put the indicated number of counters on the coloured circles. See who gets to the birthday cake first and sing 'Happy birthday to you' to the winner. A splendid addition to this game is to collect Smartie lids as counters — it makes buying sweets much more exciting.

Whose birthday?

Snakes and ladders

This can be quite difficult and frustrating for small children but they still enjoy it, especially if played with older children. You can introduce a child to the game by making your own board with only twenty-five squares.

187

Skittles

You can make your own skittles by filling — or partly filling — six plastic washing-up liquid bottles or squash bottles. Line them up and let the child roll or throw a ball to see how many he can knock down. This is not only useful for hand and eye co-ordination but is also a good counting game — 'How many have you knocked over?' Later on you can enter each score on a piece of paper and after a few throws count them all up — an introduction to basic arithmetic.

Shopping

Children begin to understand money very early! But it is still a good idea to let the tiny capitalists play around with the stuff — sorting it, counting it, working out what adds up to what. No firm advice can be given about the right age to start giving pocket money, but a few pence each week to spend or to put in a money box is a good idea from the time he makes the connection between handing over a coin and getting something back for it. 'Saving up' by keeping one week's pennies to put with another's to buy something special is an idea that can be introduced at a convenient time. Again, it is impossible to be precise about this. Paying his own fare on the bus is always fun.

Telling the time

This is much more complicated than adults ever realize and children cannot really cope until they are seven or eight years old. But young children are able to relate the position of the hands to various events during the day. Time for school. Television time. Bedtime. Daddy-come-home time. A cuckoo-clock or a striking clock makes life easier because this adds another physical dimension — the sound comes when the big hand is pointing straight up. When children can identify numbers they will be able to say that the big hand is on seven and the little hand on four but don't expect them to follow through by saying 'Twenty-five to four'. *You* can say that and they will thus begin to get used to how the times of the day sound.

You can also familiarize them with clocks by making them one of their own from a cheese box, two strips of card and a paper fastener. Cut two strips of card two inches and three inches long and cut points on them. Pierce holes at the other end and through the middle of the cheese box. Stick the fastener through 'hands' and cheesebox. Colour the 'hands' and write the hours round the face of the clock.

Clock to make

Memory games

I went out to dinner Take it in turns to say 'I went out to dinner and I ate roast beef.' 'I went out to dinner and I ate roast beef and potatoes.' 'I went out to dinner and ate roast beef, potatoes and beans', etc. A variation is 'I packed my sister's suitcase using items of clothing.' A little imagination will produce many other variations. This game can be played by one child or several.

'I spy'

Too familiar to need describing but remember it need not only be about initial letters, but can include colours, shapes, sizes, etc. Give the phonetic sound of the initial letter until you are sure that the child really grasps its ABC, e.g., 'cu' for 'cup' not 'C' for 'cup'.

Books, rhymes, songs

By the time the child starts 'big school' he should have his own little library of well-loved books which should be added to as often as his advancing needs and the housekeeping allow. This should, in fact, continue throughout his childhood, the books at the bottom end being passed onto younger children as he grows out of them. Always let him choose which books he wants to give away.

As you read to him you may find that he knows many of the stories off by heart, and he will be able to 'read' these familiar books to himself. Later he will recognize some familiar words when they appear in a different context and the way to reading has begun.

He will also begin to realize that words that rhyme usually have identical endings. This discovery tells him a great deal about spelling.

Songs are fun for him to listen to or sing. Counting songs like 'Ten green bottles' and 'One man went to mow' are popular, or even silly ones like

> Three seagulls, three seagulls
> Three seagulls, sitting on a rock
> Oh look! One's flown away! Aah!
> Two seagulls, two seagulls
> Two seagulls sitting on a rock . . .

Until

> No seagulls, no seagulls
> No seagulls, sitting on a rock
> Oh look! One's come back again! Hooray!
> One seagull, one seagull, etc.

Or

> There were ten in the bed and the little one said,
> 'Roll over! Roll over!'
> So they all rolled over and one fell out
> There were nine in the bed and the little one said,
> 'Roll! Roll over!'

and so on.

And finally a few traditional rhymes with rolling words:

> Gregory Griggs, Gregory Griggs
> Had twenty-seven different wigs
> He wore them up, he wore them down
> To please the people of the town
> He wore them east, he wore them west
> But he never could tell which he loved the best.

> Three young rats with black felt hats
> Three young ducks with white straw flats [sandals]
> Three young dogs with curling tails
> Three young cats with demi-veils
> Went out to walk with two young pigs
> In satin vests and sorrel wigs
> And suddenly it chanced to rain
> And so they all went home again.